ALSO BY MELANIE SHANKLE

Piper and Mabel: Two Very Wild but Very Good Dogs

*It's All About the Small Things: Why
the Ordinary Moments Matter
(formerly titled Church of the Small Things)*

Fearless Faith: 100 Devotions for Girls

Everyday Holy: Finding a Big God in the Little Moments

*Nobody's Cuter than You: A Memoir
about the Beauty of Friendship*

*The Antelope in the Living Room: The Real
Story of Two People Sharing One Life*

Sparkly Green Earrings: Catching the Light at Every Turn

ON THE BRIGHT SIDE

STORIES ABOUT FRIENDSHIP, LOVE, AND BEING TRUE TO YOURSELF

Melanie Shankle

ZONDERVAN®

ZONDERVAN

On the Bright Side
Copyright © 2020 by Melanie Shankle

Requests for information should be addressed to:
Zondervan, *3900 Sparks Dr. SE, Grand Rapids, Michigan 49546*

Zondervan titles may be purchased in bulk for educational, business, fundraising, or promotional use. For information, please email SpecialMarkets@Zondervan.com.

ISBN 978-0-310-34944-0 (hardcover)
ISBN 978-0-310-35839-8 (international trade paper edition)
ISBN 978-0-310-35822-0 (audio)
ISBN 978-0-310-34956-3 (ebook)

All Scripture quotations, unless otherwise indicated, are taken from The Holy Bible, New International Version®, NIV®. Copyright © 1973, 1978, 1984, 2011 by Biblica, Inc.® Used by permission of Zondervan. All rights reserved worldwide. www .Zondervan.com. The "NIV" and "New International Version" are trademarks registered in the United States Patent and Trademark Office by Biblica, Inc.®

Scripture quotations marked ESV are taken from the ESV® Bible (The Holy Bible, English Standard Version®). Copyright © 2001 by Crossway, a publishing ministry of Good News Publishers. Used by permission. All rights reserved.

Any internet addresses (websites, blogs, etc.) and telephone numbers in this book are offered as a resource. They are not intended in any way to be or imply an endorsement by Zondervan, nor does Zondervan vouch for the content of these sites and numbers for the life of this book.

The author is represented by the literary agency of Alive Literary Agency, www .aliveliterary.com.

Cover illustrations: Oleksandr Tretiachenko | Shutterstock
Interior design: Denise Froehlich

Printed in the United States of America

19 20 21 22 23 24 LSC   10 9 8 7 6 5 4 3 2 1

To Perry and Caroline
The two of you are always and
forever my brightest side

CONTENTS

INTRODUCTION

I always feel like introductions are a weird, yet necessary part of any kind of memoir-esque book. And I'm assuming that's the category this book will fall under, even though Amazon will do its best to make sure it's listed under some obscure category description, such as "Books>Self-Help>Biographies>Rhythm and Blues>Relationships with people who don't like doing crafts." This is their attempt to make sure virtually every book they sell has a chance to be a number-one bestseller in at least one category. And listen, Amazon, I appreciate that. Signed, the number-one bestselling author of a "Books>Women's Issues>Religious Humor>People with Dogs" book.

Anyway, an introduction. I never know whether to assume that you, dear reader, have read other things I have written and are kind enough to read another one of my books, or if you were just perusing the shelves at Barnes & Noble and randomly came across this book because I was in that same Barnes & Noble last week and moved it from the back of the store to a prominent table at the entrance labeled, "Our Must-Reads of the Year."

Whatever the case, let me say hello. My name is Melanie. I've been married to my husband, Perry, for over twenty-two years now. We have an only child named Caroline, who is in the midst of her teen years, which means we also serve as ATMs, fun police, child psychologists, and chauffeurs. We all live in San Antonio, Texas, with our dogs, Piper and Mabel, who are as cute as they are neurotic. Nothing in our life is extremely noteworthy. In fact, we are often in our pajamas by 6:30 at night, yet I somehow manage to find enough raw material to fill books, and for that I am grateful. Let me just say right now that I'm so glad you picked up this book, and I hope you turn the last page feeling like it was worth your time and money and, perhaps, that we would be good friends. Or at the very least, that you won't get on Amazon and give it a one-star review, Becky.

Speaking of the perils of publishing, about two years ago I was in the midst of doing publicity for a book that was about to be released. This is my least favorite part of the publishing process. And by least favorite, I mean that I would rather spend an afternoon doing craft projects that involve glitter and a group of non-potty-trained toddlers than figure out how to make people want to buy a book I've written. I hear myself during interviews or book signings, and I'm very aware that my voice rises to an octave only dogs can hear, and my Texas drawl gets even more pronounced than usual as I say, "Hiiiiiiiiiiiii! I'm so happy to be here!" And the truth is, I *am* happy to be there. I just wish I could be there and be a little quieter and less the center of attention in that particular moment. The only place I really like to be is in the center of my couch.

Anyway, publicity always means writing pieces for various magazines or online outlets along with other interviews and such, and this often includes having an excerpt from the upcoming book published in lieu of an original piece. This is basically how what I now refer to as "Hermit Crabbageddon 2017" began. I'd written what I thought was a funny little story about how my daughter, Caroline's, hermit crabs ended up being accidentally set free in our backyard, never to be seen again. I speculated that maybe they packed their teeny-tiny crab bags and set out for brighter shores and happier days after long being relegated to a plastic aquarium in our playroom. This excerpt from the book ended up being published online by a major media outlet, and I quickly found myself the most hated person in the world of hermit crab aficionados.

Did you know there are over seventy-five Facebook groups committed to rehoming unwanted hermit crabs? Neither did I, until that fateful day. Now I was being completely vilified over what I meant to be a lighthearted story full of a lot of exaggeration. People wanted to beat me up in a dark alley. Strangers who'd never met me felt free to assume that if I'd lose a hermit crab, then I was a terrible parent who didn't care about my child. It was crazy, and honestly, it freaked me out. It's not even like I'd broached a truly divisive subject, such as whether or not you think YouTube videos of cats riding Roomba vacuum cleaners are funny.

I am a person who really works to avoid controversy. I'm a lifelong people pleaser by nature, which is exacerbated by the fact that I'm a child of divorce and spent my formative years trying to make everyone happy. If figuring out a way to make tension disappear is an art form, then I am the Picasso of that skill. Every personality test I take says I'm a mediator and a peacemaker. I avoid talking about politics on the internet, I don't weigh in on Facebook controversies about homeschooling versus public school, and I'm not interested in having a theological debate with anyone at any time. If I had a life motto, it would be, *I know I can't stand the heat, so I stay out of the kitchen.*

But here's what that whole thing taught me, other than never to admit on a public platform that you let your hermit crabs run away. The world is straight-up crazy right now. We have collectively lost any chill we ever had. We are addicted to the thrill of anger and outrage and have gone to the dark side. Perhaps you've noticed. We have forgotten what it means to give a fellow human the benefit of the doubt. Not only do we all seem a little more unhinged than usual due to all the political, religious, and social upheaval, but there is actually a real thing where kids are challenging each other to eat Tide PODS and snort condoms through their nose. I don't even understand what is going on, but I feel like both of these things are indirectly referenced in the book of Revelation.

What I'm saying is, it's hard to know what's real and true anymore when we live in a world that will turn on you for accidentally setting a hermit crab free. There are so many voices shouting so many messages that we can't hear what anyone is actually saying. Who do we trust? What do we believe? What really matters? And it's like we're all so desperate to feel something that we're quick to choose anger and judgment because we'd rather feel those things than be numb. Somewhere in the midst of all of these arguments and debates and the basic ups and downs life brings, we've lost sight of what matters the most: the basic tenets of being a good person, such as kindness, gentleness, love, and mercy. We've forgotten how to be decent human beings. We've lost the art of looking on the bright side.

I mentioned earlier that we have two dogs, Piper and Mabel. They are sisters from the same litter, and we brought them home as puppies about five years ago. Our original plan was to get one puppy, but it's hard to stop at just one puppy when there are several climbing all over you with their puppy breath and paws that smell like Fritos. But here's what I will tell you about getting sister puppies from the same litter: sibling rivalry is real even in the canine world. Every morning, I sit on the couch with my cup of coffee and my laptop with Piper curled up on one side of me and Mabel curled up on the other. It's a peaceful scene until the point when Mabel decides she resents Piper's presence on the couch. Never mind that they basically descended from wolves who used to have to kill for food and who could have only dreamed of the comfort of sleeping on a leather couch with throw pillows from Pottery Barn; the fact that Mabel has to share a couch with her sister, Piper, causes her to come undone. She starts by giving her the side eye which quickly turns into a full-blown growl and snarl.

Since finding yourself in the middle of a dogfight on your couch is the complete opposite of a relaxing morning, I try to diffuse the situation by putting a large throw pillow next to Mabel so that she can't see Piper. The thing is, though, Mabel continues to crane her little doggy neck over and around the pillow to keep growling at Piper. It's like she wants to be angry. And so I find myself saying, "Quit looking at her! Stop looking at your sister! If it makes you that angry, then just look away!" This is really a life lesson for all of us. Why do we keep looking over the pillow at the very thing that triggers us? I was telling my best friend, Gulley, about how Mabel has taught me that sometimes we all need to just look away and quit growling, and she suggested that we start a movement called #BeBetterThanMabel.

This led to my vision for *On the Bright Side*. There are times when we need to take a break from looking at all that is dark and focus on the things that are bright. These are the rays of light that are often overlooked, but they can illuminate what really matters and remind us to make each day count. These are the lights that can guide us in making good decisions, choosing good friends, finding the joy life has to offer, and getting through hard times. These are the things I try to impart to Caroline as we drive to school or sit at the dinner table, because I know that it's what she will find on the bright side that will hold the key to all that she will do and all that she can become, and I pray she's listening even as she is checking Snapchat and deciding what filter to use on her streaks. There are certain principles of life and love and joy and all that is good and true in this world that never change, like remembering to treat others the way we want to be treated. It's remembering to #BeBetterThanMabel and know when to quit letting the hard things or the difficult situations or challenging family members steal our joy.

The more I think about it, the more I realize there are lessons and stories and reminders of real-life heart and decency that we can't let each other forget. These truths are the bright side of life that ensure we will never be alone and that we will live with purpose. They are meant to be shared and passed on. They help us remain true to ourselves and to who God created us to be. We will love better, live richer, and laugh more when we live on the bright side. Let's quit looking over the throw pillow and growling at each other, and instead, find the light. Our time here on this earth is incredibly short, so I'm choosing to spend it looking on the bright side. I hope you'll join me.

Love,
Melanie

CHAPTER 1

THE BRIGHT SIDE OF

FINDING YOUR PEOPLE

Each friend represents a world in us, a world possibly not born until they arrive, and it is only by this meeting that a new world is born.

—ANAÏS NIN, *THE DIARY OF ANAÏS NIN*

When I was about four years old, my mom woke up early one morning to the sound of knocking at the front door. She got out of bed to see who on earth had decided to drop by at such an unacceptable hour for visitors and found our neighbor standing at the door, holding my hand. It seems I'd woken up, gotten myself dressed, and decided to venture next door to see if my friend Margo could play. The day before, we'd launched a very lucrative business selling Hershey's Kisses wrappers we had painstakingly smoothed out, and I didn't want to waste any time before earning more cold, hard cash in what was clearly a genius venture. I guess that was before I'd discovered the glory that is sleeping late.

There are several takeaways from this childhood anecdote, probably the most important being how mortified my mom must have been to realize her child had left the house without her knowing it. But what stands out to me is that even at that young age, I was always ready to spend time with my girlfriends. This has been a constant throughout my life. I love my friends, and there have been many who have added more value and joy to my life than I could ever express in the pages of this book.

As women, I think we spend a lot of the first part of our lives dreaming about finding our Prince Charming, and we are fed an abundance of movies that focus on true love, so we buy into the idea of our soul mate being out there waiting for us. I spent several years thinking my soul mate might be George Michael from Wham!, so I clearly missed a memo on something. His hair looked so good in the music video for "Last Christmas" that we can chalk that up to an honest mistake. But when I look back over my childhood and teen years and even into adulthood, the real constant in my life has been my girlfriends. Even after being married all these years, I wonder if someone can really be our soul mate when they don't care to hear all our thoughts on the best waterproof mascara or talk about which anti-aging creams are the most effective. It's our girlfriends who remind us of the woman we were before we were a wife and a mother. It's our girlfriends who encourage and challenge us to grow into the woman God intends us to be. They see the girl in us who is still trying to figure out life and find our way in the world. They are the safe place where we can admit we don't have all the answers and we have no idea what we are doing and life feels a little scary and uncertain.

After my best friend, Gulley, had her second baby back in 2005, she was living in the haze that is trying to wrangle a toddler who thinks a couch is also a trampoline while simultaneously nursing a newborn and trying not to fall asleep standing up because she was constantly sleep deprived. And so, for her birthday that year, I decided what she probably needed most was a girls' night out. I called our mutual friend, Hilary, and she helped me put together a small group to go eat Mexican food and celebrate Gulley's birthday. There were six of us at that first dinner, and most of us didn't know each other very well or even at all, but we were all in the same stage of life: raising babies, fighting postpartum depression, trying to lose baby weight, and figuring out how to keep the spark in our marriages when we've had whiny toddlers hanging on our legs all day. It was a pretty random group, but the things we had in common bonded us together over that first batch of margaritas and chips and queso. We were all desperate for grown-up conversation and interaction that didn't involve Elmo and Mr. Noodle and having to ask someone repeatedly, "Do you need to go pee-pee?"

By the time that first dinner ended, we had already made plans to do it again the following month to celebrate my birthday. Eventually, we called ourselves the "Birthday Club" because our original purpose was to get together for each person's birthday. When our dinners out became a monthly thing, our husbands all questioned how we managed to celebrate a birthday every month of the year when there were only six of us. To which we responded, "Mind your own business."

For the next ten years, we got together on a regular basis and even upped the Birthday Club ante by taking a girls' trip each summer. We lived through pregnancies, new babies, marital struggles, potty-training nightmares, strong-willed toddlers, and all manner of family drama. We shared stories from our past and our present and talked about our dreams for the future. Those monthly dinners were the thing we looked forward to most because they were essentially free group therapy over chips and salsa.

But then our babies started to grow up, and it wasn't as easy to get our kids in pajamas and headed to bed by 7:00 p.m. so we could have a night out. There were sporting events and school programs to attend, and as life continued to get more and more busy, our monthly dinners turned into bi-monthly dinners, and then once-a-quarter dinners, and eventually we were managing to get together only once or twice a year. We'd all forgotten to prioritize the very thing that kept us sane and grounded.

Last summer, as it got closer to my birthday, I realized the thing I wanted most was to get together with Birthday Club. Gulley sent out a group text, and we all agreed on a time and place to meet for dinner. And even though it had been a while since we'd all been together, we immediately fell back into our same shorthand and closeness. Because we all have a tendency to talk fast and furiously in an attempt to cover every bit of conversational ground, we started a practice many years ago that we call, "Pinky up!" This just means that we are briefly tabling a new thought that just occurred to us while still discussing our original thought. Saying "Pinky up!" is a verbal reminder to circle back around so we don't forget to cover whatever that topic happens to be. For example, "Pinky up! When you mentioned those cute sandals you found at Target, I just remembered I need to tell you about what happened in the carpool line at school the other day" or "Pinky up! Speaking of postpartum pregnancy underwear, I just realized we haven't talked about Meghan Markle's post-birth photo shoot and if we think there really is a feud between the Sussex and Cambridge families." As we sat around that dinner table eating a mix of roasted brussels sprouts and parmesan fries, there were more pinkies-up than I could count, and I could almost hear the collective sigh of relief that comes from being with people who just get you.

Our kids are almost all teenagers now, and if there is ever a time in your life when you need to air it all out and get real about things, it's when you are raising teenagers. There is no handbook or guide. There is no one right answer. We all agreed that the dirty little secret no one tells you about having teenagers is that none of us know what the heck we are doing. It's a precarious, humbling time in life when you find yourself trying to teach children to drive while simultaneously wondering why your hands are starting to look like your grandmother's and how you can increase the font size on your text messages so you can actually see the text from the child you carried in your womb for nine months that says, "GTG TTYL" (Got to go. Talk to you later).

By the end of that dinner, we all renewed our commitment to get together on a regular basis, no matter what we had to do to make it happen. We left that night a little lighter in that way you feel when you realize you aren't alone and, even better, that maybe you're actually not crazy. It's that feeling you get when you remember you have people who would do anything in the world for you and for whom you'd do the same, which sometimes looks a whole lot like just listening and understanding and not judging when you share that you flipped the bird at your child behind his back as he stomped into his room. We'd gotten so busy being busy that we'd forgotten to make friendship a priority, and that dinner was the reset button we all needed to remember the things that brought us together in the first place. We've lived up to our promises, bringing back our girls' weekend this summer, and we have gotten together more often, even in the midst of all the other things we have going on, because it's worth it. People talk all the time about self-care, and I believe one of the biggest things we can do to take care of ourselves is spend time with friends who make us feel normal.

Here's the thing about Birthday Club that snuck up on me. When we first started getting together all those years ago, it felt hard to open up and make new friends. I'm a person who likes my old friends. I like the familiar and the comfortable. But over the course of all those dinners, I opened up little by little, and eventually I looked up and realized that my new friends had become old friends. We have lived a lot of life together, but every friendship has to have a starting point.

We can trick ourselves into believing we're doing okay on our own for a while, but eventually, I believe we all circle back to how much we need people who know us and love us in real life. Seasons of life change, but the need for ride-or-die friends never does. They represent some of the very best stuff that life has to offer.

✳ ✳ ✳

Last fall, I traveled to Marshall, Texas, to speak at a women's event. This meant I got to fly into the bustling East Texas Regional Airport. It only has one gate. The entire airport is essentially the size of my living room. On the upside, this meant I was able to walk five feet to the rental car counter as opposed to the fifty-mile shuttle ride required to reach the Hertz counter when you fly into the Dallas/Fort Worth airport. Not even O. J. Simpson would be able to rent a car quickly at Dallas/Fort Worth. Is it too soon to make an O. J. Simpson joke? I'm going to go with no.

I walked up to the rental car counter, and the clerk said, "Honey, let me see what cars we got in right now," as she opened up a drawer and pulled out three sets of keys. She turned to her co-worker lounging in a chair behind her and asked, "Don, how's that VW Beetle?" Don sat up with the realization he was being called into action and replied, "Well, it's okay. It's got something hanging down underneath it that drags as you drive, but I don't reckon it'll hinder you none."

This isn't really the type of rental car security and safety I'm looking for when I travel alone to speaking events. What if Don is wrong, and it hinders me to a great degree in the form of getting stuck on the side of a road in East Texas? I voiced this concern, and Don offered to follow me out to the lot to check out the VW Beetle before I got on the road. He even wheeled my suitcase out there for me, loaded it in the car, and then lay flat on his back to shimmy under the car and check out the offending car part that was dragging on the ground. And to Don's utter delight, he was able to just break that piece of plastic off the car and eliminate the dragging. Was I a little concerned about whether or not that piece of plastic might be a crucial component of the car? Sure. But I felt like Don had offered up exceptional customer service in the form of rudimentary auto repair, so I drove the VW Beetle to my hotel, and all was well. Don was right. It did, in fact, hinder me none.

As soon as I arrived at the hotel, I called home to check in with my people, and that's when I found out that Caroline had had a terrible day at school. There were tears, and it was one of those moments when I wished desperately that I wasn't so far away. It's hard to know your child is hurting and not be able to be there, and this was the breaking point of an ongoing situation that had brought us all to the end of our patience. I left for my speaking event shortly after I got off the phone with Caroline and got through the first session of my talk without incident. But when I began speaking during the second session, I got to a point where I talk about life not always turning out like we hope, and I found myself in tears. I had to stop in an attempt to compose myself, and I ended up sharing what was going on in our lives and how hard it was to watch Caroline struggle. It was a moment when I went from being semi-scripted to being totally raw and vulnerable. I felt like I was on stage in my underwear.

But you know what happened? One sweet woman jumped up from the front row and brought me a pack of Kleenex, another one grabbed me a water bottle, and I could feel that something in that church sanctuary had shifted. In that moment of unplanned honesty and emotion, God entered in, and everything got real. The women in that church will have my heart forever because they were there for me. After my talk was over, I lost count of how many of them came up to hug me, share their own stories, encourage me, and tell me they would be praying for my family. They had become friends. We all showed each other our true selves, all the ways we felt broken, and were stronger for it on the other side because we realized that none of us were alone.

When I got home, I pulled the little pack of Kleenex out of my purse and noticed that the custom label on it read, "Happy Tears." I thought of the kindness those women showed me and knew that while mine weren't necessarily happy tears, God had made them holy tears. It was a reminder of how awesome it can be when we remember that we're all in this life together and that being real always outweighs pretending you have it all figured out. That's what happens when women feel safe with each other. Those are the moments when friendship begins.

I believe one of the most important things we need to pass down to the girls who are growing up after us is the beauty of female friendship and what it adds to our lives. We need to teach them that we need people who will listen to our stories and be there for us as we go through heartbreak and joy and figure out everything life throws our way. We all need loyal soldiers who will defend us and stand with us when times get hard and it feels like the world is against us, because it seems that we're creating a generation with a tendency to substitute the joy of real friendship with cheap imitations, such as community on Facebook or Instagram, or friendship via text messages that allow us to communicate with someone without a face-to-face commitment. We swim in the pool of shallow relationships because we all know that going deep requires being vulnerable. It's so much easier to just text someone the praying hands emoji than it is to actually take the time to listen and hear what's going on. And maybe, for a while, that feels like real community. Until it doesn't.

We all need people who will show up on our doorsteps with fajitas and cookies and Kleenex when the hard times come. And we all need to be that person for someone. We need people in our lives who can look into our eyes and ask if we're okay when they already know we're not. Our friends are what make life worth living and remind us we are never alone.

Almost three years ago, I lost one of my oldest and dearest friends to breast cancer. Jen was one of the strongest and most faith-filled people I have ever known. She lived just about eighteen months after finding out her cancer had spread and that the odds were against recovery. During that time, those of us in her circle of friends spent more time together than we had in years because there was a sense of urgency to make the most of the time we had left. We fit as much love and laughter and tears and truths as we possibly could into what felt like an increasingly small window. And Jen never stopped showing up for us. Even when she was at one of her lowest points, she talked our friend Jamie into making the five-hour drive to San Antonio with her to be at the launch party for my book, *Nobody's Cuter Than You*.

That night, our whole group of friends was together for what turned out to be the last time, and it will go down as one of my most precious memories. We howled with laughter because, when Perry went to leave my book signing that night, he hugged Jen and said, "Jen, I guess I won't be seeing you again," meaning he knew she was leaving early the next morning to head back to Dallas while he would already be at work. Without missing a beat, she looked at him and replied, "Put that in the category of things you don't say to someone with terminal cancer." She never quit making us laugh. And she taught us all how to love better.

When Gulley and I got the call that we should get to Dallas to see Jen during what appeared to be the beginning of the end, we immediately jumped in the car and made the drive. Caroline wanted to come with us, and several hours later, we were sitting in Jen's hospital room. She was on a lot of pain medication, and we weren't sure if she would even wake up and know we were there, but she did. We were able to talk for a little while and share a few laughs and tears. I was so thankful my daughter was there to witness this holy moment of friendship, because it is the very marrow of life, the kind of moment that really matters.

Then it was time to leave. We all knew what this goodbye meant. I can't even write about it now without tears rolling down my face. Jen had been a part of our lives for the last twenty-five years. We'd all grown up together. We met at Texas A&M, and we watched each other graduate, move away, move back home, get married, have babies, lose parents, rediscover our faith, and survive heartbreaks. We'd eaten countless amounts of raw chocolate chip cookie dough curled up on couches everywhere from College Station to San Antonio to Dallas. Our lives had intersected when we were nineteen, and we had been to one another the very air we all needed in order to survive the ensuing years. How do you say goodbye to a relationship like that?

Jen had her eyes closed as we got ready to leave, and we hugged her and told her through tears how much she was loved, and she said, "I don't want to open my eyes because then I'll know I'm seeing you for the last time." I whispered, "It's not goodbye. It's *I'll see you later*," because I do know we will see each other again where there are no tears and no cancer, and the laughter and cookie dough will flow like milk and honey.

While Jen was in the middle of losing her fight with cancer, she wrote these words about Moses and the children of Israel crossing the Red Sea.

> I couldn't imagine how the Israelites ran headlong toward the sea, not knowing if it would open, yet trusting the Lord to deliver them. I thought about how if the sea had parted two hundred yards before they arrived, it wouldn't have required the same faith. I admire them. And I thought of how I feel like people give me too much credit for joy and peace and grace in this season, but that it's truly *he* who has opened the seas and provided a smooth path in the face of death. And I've seen him provide supernatural peace and grace. Until I was willing to step all the way up to the water's edge (or he walked me to the edge), I couldn't experience the sweetness of this "deliverance" into joy that completely overwhelms me.

None of us wants to walk right up to the water's edge of the painful seasons in our life without knowing if God is going to part the seas. We prefer to know in advance what is happening and where we are going and that we are going to be okay. But I believe as we take those baby steps of trusting God with what is right in front of us—in this hour, then this day, then the next day, and then the next week—we will come to realize that no matter how difficult things are, he sees us. He's like a proud dad watching a toddler finding her footing, cheering us on because he knew we had it in us all along. We were the ones who didn't know.

And you know what I love as you get to Exodus 15, right after the Israelites crossed through the Red Sea on dry land against all natural and human odds? It says, "For when the horses of Pharaoh with his chariots and his horsemen went into the sea, the LORD brought back the waters of the sea upon them, but the people of Israel walked on dry ground in the midst of the sea. Then Miriam the prophetess, the sister of Aaron, took a tambourine in her hand, and all the women went out after her with tambourines and dancing" (Exodus 15:19–20 ESV).

Moses and the people of Israel had fled from Egypt. They were being pursued by the greatest army in the world at that time. They had no idea where they were going or how they were going to make it through to the other side. I can't even imagine their fear and panic, the certainty that they were all surely about to die at the hands of Pharaoh's army. They were living a nightmare. But then God *does* deliver them to the other side and Miriam and *all the women* get out their tambourines and begin to dance.

Think about what that means. It means that in the midst of what had to be the scariest time of uncertainty they had ever faced, they packed their tambourines. Because, yes, they were afraid and, no, this wasn't their plan, but they trusted God, so they packed their tambourines. They believed and trusted that a day would come when they would dance and rejoice again. And you know who led the dancing? *All the women.*

Life can bring some heartaches that just won't fully heal, and we will have struggles we didn't anticipate. We will question the way we mother, the way we live, the decisions we make, and whether or not we are up for the task at hand. We will struggle with anxiety, depression, insignificance, and whether or not it's okay to email a teacher to ask about our kid's bad grade on a test. We will all walk up to a version of the water's edge many times in our lives, but when we are surrounded by the women we count as friends, they will help us remember to pack our tambourines. Because life will bring us down, but the women who walk it out with us are the ones who will give us the strength to dance again. They will cry with us when we need to cry, they will hold our hands through the worst of it, and then they will pass out the tambourines when it's time to get up and live again.

The bright side is knowing that our lives are forever changed for the better by the women God gives us to walk with through life, to be each other's greatest cheerleaders, encouragers, teachers, and tambourine players.

CHAPTER 2

THE BRIGHT SIDE OF
GIVING UP ON COMPARING AND COMPETING

To be yourself in a world that is constantly trying to make you something else is the greatest accomplishment.

—RALPH WALDO EMERSON

When Caroline was in junior high, she decided to join the band. This came as a surprise to Perry and me because we had never known her to show interest in anything musical. It made much more sense when she announced that the band got to take an end-of-the-school-year trip to Schlitterbahn Water Park. If she had told us that up front, we could have saved a lot of money on a flute rental and just taken her to Schlitterbahn instead. Of course, then we would've missed that parental rite of passage known as the sixth-grade band concert, and that would've been a real tragedy.

As the school year went on, she repeatedly complained about being in the band and, specifically, being last chair for the entire flute section. But here's the thing: she *never once* brought her flute home to practice. We finally had to have one of those tough love talks and point out that she was not going to learn to play the flute by osmosis. It was going to require hard work and practice, and we would support her in all of that if the flute was her passion, but if that wasn't the case, then maybe it was time to find another activity. Apparently, the allure of a trip to Schlitterbahn wasn't as strong after she realized the work involved, and she ultimately quit. But that failure, that moment of honesty, allowed her to figure out what she did care about and what other strengths she could build on. She chose instead to use her fine arts elective for a theater class and learned that she loved helping to build sets and design costumes.

We have to be honest with our kids about what it takes to succeed, then figure out how to guide them in their natural gifts. Which leads me to Caroline's dance career—and by "career," I mean a terrible idea I once had.

When Caroline was three years old, I was prepared to fulfill my lifelong dream of having a daughter who regularly performed in dance recitals. I think some of this was born out of my own short-lived ballet career, which didn't produce any real dancing fruit but is the reason there is a darling picture of four-year-old me in a tiara and a gorgeous pink tutu, with a cascade of long, brown curls flowing down my back. Truth be told, from the time the sonogram confirmed we were having a girl, I envisioned that photograph of myself and assumed that was exactly who and what my daughter would be. I would get to mother a delicate little girl in a dreamy pink tutu and precious little ballet slippers. As it turns out, that is not what God had planned for me. However, I didn't fully know that the day I signed Caroline up for dance lessons, which is why I paid for everything—an entire year of classes, the recital, and recital costume—in advance.

To this day, it's one of the dumbest things I've ever done. Every week was like a scene out of the book of Job as I bargained and pled with her to just make it through the class. She hated it. She hated that she had to be quiet, she hated wearing the required pink leotard, and she hated that she couldn't just run around the classroom and listen to the sound of her feet on the wooden dance floor. Yet, I persisted because WE HAD PAID FOR THE YEAR IN ADVANCE. And I wanted a picture of her in her recital costume. Would it have been easier to just go buy a tutu and have a photograph taken? Yes, it would have. I can't tell you how sorry I am that I didn't think of that at the time.

Finally, after months of dance class agony, it was time for the recital. Caroline didn't necessarily love the costume, but she did love the makeup she was allowed to wear, so that was her incentive to go through with the dance routine. I stood backstage with all the other moms and their tiny, graceful ballerinas with bows that actually stayed straight in their hair, as opposed to Caroline's, which insisted on cocking to one side. The little girls all filed out onto the stage to begin their rehearsed dance number and I watched from the audience as Caroline did the occasional move but mainly just smiled and waved to us in the crowd and stomped her feet while she did more of a march-in-a-circle move as opposed to a graceful twirl. Yet as soon as we found her backstage, she declared loudly, "I won! I beat all those other girls!" And that's when we realized that maybe a sport of some kind was going to be her thing. Due to her boundless energy, soccer seemed to make the most sense, and so we entered the world of youth sports, full of hope and optimism for all the ways it would enrich our daughter and teach her valuable life lessons.

And I have to say, soccer hasn't let us down. It's been a keeper. No extra charge for that soccer-related pun.

The irony of raising a daughter who has such a competitive spirit is that I have never really considered myself to be a competitive person. I'm not sure if this is just a personality characteristic that's not inherent in some people, or because I never pursued any kind of athletic endeavor that lent itself to wanting to win. This is what happens when you spend your entire elementary school career being picked last for high jump or dodgeball. And

I'll be the first to own the fact that I would've picked me last, too. When it comes to the dog-eat-dog world of third-grade physical education, no one wants the kid who is really funny and sarcastic but can't manage to clear a two-foot hurdle on the high jump team.

Of course, there was one time in fifth grade when I actually did see a little competitive streak surface in myself. My team lost a closely contested softball game. I felt that the coach had given the opposing team an extra run they hadn't earned, and quickly found myself in the principal's office for challenging the coach by saying, "Three plus one equals four, and if you don't know that then maybe you should go back to the fifth grade." Please note here that I said I was the funny, sarcastic kid, not the smart kid.

I have spent most of my life believing I'm just not a competitive person, unless it involves a round of Trivial Pursuit or watching a Texas A&M sporting event. I've always been more in the vein of Patty Simcox in *Grease*, saying, "I just hope we don't make too poor a showing," or "Who cares who wins some stupid card game?" This is interesting considering how much I am like my dad in so many ways. He once threw his hand of cards directly at a boy I was dating because he lost at a round of gin rummy. Maybe the competitive gene skips a generation.

However, something interesting has happened over the last ten or so years. Enter social media, stage right. All of a sudden, I had a way to compare and contrast my life with other people's lives. I didn't have to wait until a high school reunion to see how my life trajectory compared with those of my classmates because I could go on Facebook and immediately learn that their kids were all on the honor roll, they just bought a new Mercedes, their husband recently got a promotion, and the whole family was going to the Amalfi Coast over the summer to stay at a little place they'd purchased. (Actually, this is an exaggeration, because if I really knew this person, then I wouldn't mock them in my book, but would embrace them because they own a place on the Amalfi Coast and summer with George and Amal Clooney, and perhaps they might invite me to join them.)

When Caroline was almost four years old, I made a career change. I transitioned out of pharmaceutical sales—where I had never had one competitive urge to increase my drug's market share over that of my colleagues, in spite of all the incentive programs that were created in the hope that we'd all begin to sell allergy medicine like it was a competition on *American Ninja Warrior*—into writing. Being in publishing gave me access to a world in which I was fortunate enough to befriend other female writers and speakers walking the same road but which also meant I had to think about things like "platform" and "building my social media reach." Enter Instagram, stage left. I suddenly had a front row seat to every speaking and writing opportunity these women had. I could view in real time what events I hadn't been asked to be a part of or what writing compilations no one asked me to contribute to. I could view Insta-stories that were witty and brilliant marketing pieces for someone's latest project or conference at a time when I still wasn't even sure how to hit record for an Insta-story and actually went live by accident one time, during which, thankfully, I did nothing but record a live look at my kitchen floor for twenty seconds. It was as compelling as you might imagine.

Now my life and career kind of felt like a party I wanted to be invited to, even if I wasn't sure I wanted to attend. I began to question why no one was asking me to speak at this event or that thing. Why wasn't I worthy of contributing a piece to that website or magazine? Was it because I was funny but not spiritual enough? Was it because I was *too* spiritual? Was it because I was more conservative than other people? Was it because sometimes my teeth look enormous when I smile?

That's when I realized I had prided myself on not giving in to comparison or competition, but the truth was, I just hadn't discovered my competitive hot button yet. Without warning, I was drowning in comparison and competitiveness. And I didn't like that about myself. It's depressing when you've spent a lot of your life thinking you were better than you actually turn out to be.

✳ ✳ ✳

All these years later, we are solidly a soccer family. And so, I guess that makes me a soccer mom. This was not a career option I remember being represented at any sort of career day I attended during college (complete with a portable folding chair and laundry that smells like Satan's bath towel), but make no mistake, it *is* a job. I feel like my whole life can be summed up by these five words: "I can't. We have soccer." But here's the truth, I wouldn't trade it for anything in the world.

Interestingly enough, my battle with comparison happened to coincide with the time Caroline was entering the world of competitive sports. I may not have ever really cared if I won at something when I was younger, but man, did I want my child to win. I didn't want to see her overlooked or underestimated. I wanted to see her win, or at least be the best at whatever she was doing. Needless to say, when I finally had a talk with myself after one especially bad day—when I found myself resenting other people who had no idea we were even in a competition—it was a humbling, ugly moment. I had to deal with it head-on because comparison and competition cease to be healthy when they do nothing but make you feel like what you have isn't enough.

Watching Caroline on the soccer field has been one of the great joys of my life, and in no way could I ever have prepared myself for what youth sports have taught me. I need to be a mom in the stands who can make it to the end of the season still proud of who I am, of my behavior, and of the words that have come out of my mouth. Watching my child play a sport brings out a side of me I didn't even know existed. I had no idea I could feel so strongly about a referee and a bad call. I didn't know watching my child be pushed around by a competitor could make me feel so angry. I didn't know I could feel like fighting an opposing team's fans for being so obnoxious. Welcome to youth sports, where the kids are competitors and the parents can come a little undone. And by undone, I mean I've watched referees send grown men to their cars during the middle of a game because they were out of control watching a bunch of eight-year-olds chase a ball down the field.

As the mom of an athlete, this is what I make sure my daughter knows above all else: I love watching her play soccer. I love watching her run, I love watching her celebrate with teammates, and I love seeing that she gets back up when she falls down. It's not about the winning or the losing (although, let's not lie, winning is much more fun), it's about watching my child do something she is passionate about, something that makes her feel strong and capable. Because no matter how good she is or what level she eventually attains in her sport, there will come a day when her athletic career will be over. This is why it's important to make sure we are raising good, kind people and not just great athletes.

Playing a sport is a great vehicle to equip our kids for life, but only if we're letting them learn all the lessons that come with it, both good and bad. Kindness matters. Good sportsmanship matters. Respect for coaches, officials, competitors, and team-mates matters. These are things that cannot and should not be overlooked, no matter how athletically gifted my child may be. I want her to know that you shake people's hands, you look them in the eye, and you say, "Good game," even if it didn't go the way you hoped it would. You support your teammates even if they are shining brighter than you are, because one person's suc-cess doesn't diminish your own. There are spiritual lessons all throughout the mix about fighting the good fight and using the talents and abilities God has given you.

Over the years, we've been fortunate enough to have coaches who have instilled these important qualities in Caroline, but at the end of the day, it's my responsibility as a mother to lead the way, to show her what matters most, and to make sure I'm setting the example as I sit in the stands and cheer her on.

Even if I sometimes have to bite my lip until it bleeds.

I'm learning that there's a big difference between legitimate com-petition and unhealthy comparison. When I watch Caroline and her teammates fight to win a game, it reminds me of how much we can accomplish when we put aside our differences and work together. Her club soccer team is composed of girls from all over the city who have different backgrounds and histories, who come from different races and religions, but not one bit of that matters to them because they are a team. They want to win, and they know they can't do it alone. They cheer each other on and are the first ones to run over and check on a teammate who's hurt. When we travel, they pile up in hotel rooms like a litter of puppies, and you can't tell which legs belong to whom. They share everything from shin guards to secrets. They curl each other's hair and borrow each other's clothes and support each other's dreams. They may occasionally annoy one another, but make no mistake about it, they root for each other to succeed because they have realized what too many grown women still haven't—that a victory for one is a victory for all.

Watching Caroline compete has helped me reframe what is—and isn't—a legitimate competition. When I pit myself against other people or run after other women's achievements, no one wins. Comparison and feeling like everything other people have is better than what I have only serves to diminish the things God is doing in my life. There is no finite number of successful marriages or pregnancies or job promotions or kids on the honor roll. Another woman's good news doesn't limit what God wants to do in my life.

The truth is, making comparisons and allowing myself to feel like everything is a competition will just flat-out steal my joy. I love Pinterest, Instagram, and Facebook. I do. Twitter, you and your angry mob mentality can go away, but give me pictures of people's dogs all day long on Instagram. Pinterest, help me figure out ways to wear that black leather jacket I bought on a whim because it was 25 percent off. Facebook, let me know what my high school classmates are up to from a safe, no-small-talk-required distance. You complete me and are the reason I was able to say no to going on a cruise for my thirtieth high school reunion.

But here's the issue with social media. We can kill ourselves with the *I should have*s, *I could have*s, and *I wish I had*s. Yes, Cindy, I see that you keep an immaculate home and pack healthy, sensible lunches in a Bento box, and you all just spent a lovely week on the slopes at Deer Valley, where your children were such angels that even the ski patrol commented on their stellar behavior and excellent skiing ability. Good for you. I had to tell my daughter that Houston is the new Deer Valley because we're saving up for college and our spring break will include a trip to The Galleria to shop, if she's lucky.

We've been fed the idea that it benefits our kids to constantly be in their faces asking, "What do you need, my precious, wonderful noodle? How can I make your childhood amazing?" The truth is, it's never been a parent's job to make childhood magical. It already *is* magical. They get summers off, and someone makes dinner for them every night. *That's magical.* As adults, that's what we refer to as *vacation*. None of us who were born before 2001 had an Elf on the Shelf who took marshmallow baths every night leading up to Christmas Eve, and we might be better for it.

It's all just too much pressure. And I am guilty of buying into it. I drank the Instagram Kool-Aid and it tasted like Fashion Blogger who wears a size XXS in everything she features. Okay, sometimes she has to size up to an XS. "Guys! This sweater is a 00 because I wanted it oversized." But what I try to remember as I wrestle with how to handle that ugly part of me that wants to compare is that it all comes down to whether or not I believe God has me exactly where he needs me to be and, ultimately, at a place I wouldn't trade if I could—even though it can sometimes feel monotonous.

What exactly is it that I'm chasing when I start the whole comparison game?

Some days I have to have a talk with myself in order to remember that I'm in a season of life wherein I don't really want to vacation on the Amalfi Coast or be part of the latest big speaking tour because I don't want to miss what's going on in my real life. Is it glamorous? Not really. Unless you consider driving around a bunch of teenage girls who never tire of saying, "Road work ahead? I sure hope it does," to be glamorous. I spend a lot of time traveling to soccer games and cheering while I'm either freezing cold or dying a slow death from the heat. I'm picking up Caroline from school and cherishing those few minutes in the car when maybe she'll tell me about her day and what's going on in her life. I'm staying up until the wee hours of the morning writing this book because it's the only time my mind can actually focus. I'm cooking dinner and going to the grocery store and living what is, by all accounts, a pretty non-Instagrammable life.

But what God has shown me—and continues to remind me of on the days when I struggle with comparison—is that all the things I'm doing right now matter more than any bestselling book or cool speaking engagement ever could. Most of my days aren't necessarily anything people envy because they are just the stuff of real life, but after really working through it all over the last few years, I've come to realize what a gift it is to know there's nowhere else I'd rather be than in a car with a teenage girl rolling her eyes at me because she can't even believe how embarrassing it is that I told one of her friends that I was "shook."

Paying more attention to what someone else is doing—rather

than to what God is doing in my life—causes me to feel unsettled and discontented and bitter quicker than anything else. And we have an enemy who is smart enough to know that if he can discourage us enough, we may just decide to quit—to quit pursuing that thing or that calling God has planned for us so that we can take up a hobby of feeling sorry for ourselves.

This generation coming up behind us needs to see us supporting our friends, not competing or setting up an atmosphere of constant comparison and competition. That is not how we want them to view the world. Peers become competitors instead of friends. They need the grown-ups to act like grown-ups, and sometimes I think all the grown-ups have forgotten how.

I read an article a while back that said from the time a girl turns thirteen until the time she turns forty, it's essentially all downhill in terms of her contentment and happiness, a slow and steady decline. Apparently thirteen is the age when you really start to pay attention to how you compare to others, and I believe junior high social politics across the world confirm this fact. The article went on to say that a woman's best chance of being contented doesn't come until she's seventy-four. We need to do better than this.

When I struggle, it's usually not because of the specifics of my circumstances so much as a failure to trust in God's goodness to me. Deep down, I struggle to believe that God has what is best for me. It's why I want to control my own life and my own narrative instead of surrendering to vulnerability and being real.

Everything we need, everything we are supposed to be or achieve, everything our marriages are supposed to be, everything we want for our kids, everything we want for our careers or our lives, we already possess in Jesus Christ. And just because there are times when none of these things looks the way we thought they would doesn't mean God isn't working them together for our ultimate good.

We need to encourage each other—and ourselves—to be the best version of who God has called us to be, cheer each other on in our victories and successes, and be honest with each other when we have failed and feel inadequate. That's how we build a solid foundation for real relationships and remember that God has far more interesting things for each of us to do with our lives than to spend our time comparing and competing with someone else. There isn't a prize for first place in life. At least, there wasn't the last time I checked. But when we choose being real over pretending like we have it all figured out? Then, I think, we all win. There is room for every single one of us in this world.

You know how else we win? By thinking twice before we pay for a year of dance lessons and a recital in advance.

And also, maybe by avoiding Instagram when we're already having a bad day.

On the bright side, you are exactly who and what you were created to be.

CHAPTER 3

THE BRIGHT SIDE OF
FINDING YOURSELF
IN THE MIDDLE

*The really frightening thing about
middle age is that you know you'll
grow out of it.*

—DORIS DAY

Last summer, I drove to Dallas for a speaking event. Caroline came with me because I lured her with the promise that it could also be a shopping trip, which is the universal love language of teen girls. She's also savvy enough to know that when I'm asked to speak at a ladies' brunch at a church, there will most likely be good food involved. Maybe even chocolate crepes.

We rolled our luggage to the front reception desk to check into our hotel room for the night, and the desk clerk began to make conversation with us. She asked where we were from and then asked, "Why are y'all in town tonight?"

"I'm speaking at a church event tomorrow," I said.

"That's nice," she responded. "Do you write books as well?"

I was surprised she knew those two things usually go hand in hand. I didn't know until after my first book was published that people make the assumption that if you write books, then you must be able to speak in public. This has always felt like a bold assumption to me.

Anyway, I told her that I did write books as well, and she replied, "Oh, I used to write books and travel and speak, too, but then my kids went off to college and I didn't have anything to write or talk about anymore, and now I work here."

It sent cold chills down my spine. Lord, have mercy on me, a writer who wants to continue to have things to write about.

In fact, I barely made it to my hotel room before I texted my beloved literary agent and friend and said, "Please don't let me end up working the front desk at a mid-level hotel chain." Not because there is one thing wrong with being a desk clerk at a hotel, but because as much as I complain about writing books, I want to keep doing it forever and don't want to go back to working in the corporate world in any capacity now that I know what it's like to have a job that allows me to be creative and do what I love. I am painfully aware that I got my start writing a "mommy blog" full of funny stories about my child who is now only about two years away from leaving for college, and then what? Does anyone want to read a blog about dogs? Can you become a fashion blogger if all you ever wear are sweatpants and a T-shirt that says, "Texas, Come Hell or High Water"? Can you write a healthy living blog if you eat Takis on a regular basis and consider a spoonful of peanut butter a healthy breakfast?

It was just another reminder that I am in what feels like an odd, middle place of life—I'm somewhere between young motherhood and the end of the years with a child at home. Beginnings are exciting, and endings can be interesting because they usually signal the culmination of a journey or maybe a new beginning. But the middle just feels not great, Bob. I don't even think that at forty-seven years old I can actually say I'm middle-aged, unless I'm going for the gold as an optimist about my life span.

I look in the mirror and see skin that doesn't look like it used to, no matter how many products I use, the back of my thighs hurt my feelings, my metabolism is clearly trying to mock me as payback for how hard I made it work for the last forty years, my hips hurt when I get out of bed in the morning, and my hormones don't even have the courtesy to let me know if we're having a bad day until it's too late, and I snap at Caroline or Perry for turning on the heat in the house when it's only 37 degrees outside. "Can you see your breath standing here in the living room? No? Then don't turn on the heat."

I get in the car and can't decide if I want to listen to KONO 101, the local oldies station that now plays songs I danced to at my senior prom, or if I want to turn on 96.1 for today's hits and learn the words to the newest Post Malone song in a sad attempt to impress Caroline, who will just roll her eyes anyway. The other day, we were in the car listening to her Spotify playlist. A song came on, and I said casually, "Oh, is this 'Japanese Denim'?" and she said, "*Yes!*" and seemed so genuinely shocked and proud that I knew the song that I didn't have the heart to tell her it was only because I read it on the digital display on my car stereo.

The thing no one tells you about growing older is that you don't necessarily feel any different than you ever did. I remember when Gulley's family moved Nena into an assisted living home. She was eighty-eight years old, and she complained about having to live with "a bunch of old people." I laughed then, but I get it now. I got home from a meeting the other day and was describing who was there to Perry and said, "It was really just a bunch of older, middle-aged moms," and he looked at me and said, "You're an older, middle-aged mom."

Which is just rude.

But true.

It's this place in life that finds me trying to figure out how to raise a teenager and cope with the realization that I'm going to blink and be an empty nester. All I ever wanted in life was to be a mom, and this season of life with a child at home has gone by so fast that it doesn't even seem fair. She was a toddler yesterday, and we'll be filling out her college applications tomorrow. Why is my infant driving a car? I remember rocking her when she was a baby and calculating that she'd graduate from high school in 2021. That wasn't even a year I could fathom because it seemed so far away, and we'd probably all be living in spaceships by then. Maybe Jesus would return, and I wouldn't have to worry about sending my child off to the real world. But now, spoiler alert, we are almost there.

The other night, Perry and I were discussing Caroline's schedule and figuring out when she had soccer games and what nights one of us needed to pick her up from somewhere and how we had to teach her to have more respect for our time and to not keep us waiting. He said, "I told her the other day that her time is the *least valuable* of anyone who lives in our house." I complained that she is the worst about not properly closing the Doritos bag and putting it back in the pantry, her closet is a wreck, she leaves her dirty clothes and shoes wherever she happens to take them off, and her clean laundry is piled in stacks all over her room. I concluded with, "She only talks to us when she feels like it, she thinks we are at her beck and call, she never remembers to take her soccer cleats out of her backpack to air out, she tells us she's ready to go and then makes us wait on her, and she thinks we have nothing better to do with our time." Then I got teary and said, "I'm going to be so sad when it's over."

The worst thing kids do is grow up, turn into lovely people you genuinely adore, and then move out of your house. Yet the alternative is a Big and Little Edie situation straight out of *Grey Gardens*, and you certainly don't want that. If for no other reason than you could end up with raccoons living in your house.

Nothing prepares you for this point in life. Perry and I worked with teenagers for years when we were younger, so I really thought I'd have a lot more answers. But it turns out I don't, and I find that so disappointing. Back when we were in our twenties and working with Campus Life at the local high school, the parents of one of the teenage girls who regularly came to our meetings stopped by our house. They were worried about their daughter and some of the decisions she was making, and wanted to know if we had any encouragement or insight to offer. I remember being flattered but also thinking I had no idea what to tell them, and they were at least in their late thirties and had to know more than us. Now I realize they most likely didn't know more than us and were just winging it, like the rest of us do during this stage. It reminds me of a post a friend of mine from high school put on his Facebook page during a hurricane warning in his town. It was a picture of a completely empty bread aisle at a grocery store, and he wrote, "Folks want to say they're gluten-free and all that, but when a storm is coming, it looks like everybody be eatin' toast." You think you have all the answers until reality hits, and then you feel desperate and start reaching for the toast.

I didn't have Caroline until I was thirty-two, so I got a later start on kids than some of my friends. But I still feel shocked when I see on Facebook that one of them has a child who's graduating from college or getting married or, worst of all, having a baby. We all watched *Sixteen Candles* together a million times and laughed and made fun of Sam's out-of-touch grandparents, and now you're telling me that some of us actually *are* grandparents? What is even going on? Is Jake Ryan a grandpa now? This thought puts me deep in my feelings.

It's humbling to find myself at I-have-to-watch-*The-Crown*-with-subtitles-to-catch-all-the-dialog years old. And no matter how much my older friends try to assure me that the empty nest years will be great, I still feel sad when I think about it.

The truth is that life moves faster than a Chick-fil-A drive-thru during lunch hour, and this middle place of life makes me feel like the chikin.

On the other end of the spectrum is the reality that my parents are getting older. So many of my friends are either currently dealing with aging parents or have lost a parent over the last few years. It's made me realize that our parents are no longer at an age when you can say, "Oh, that's so tragic. They were so young." Alex, I'll take "Other Things I Am Not Emotionally Prepared to Handle" for $200.

But here's the thing about life—there are things God can only teach us as we go. Our whole lives are journeys with beginnings, middles, and ends. We worry about whatever the next stage of life is that feels too uncertain, because it's in those middle places that we often experience the heartbreak and hard times of life. But if we are willing to stop and look, it's in those same middle places that we will see God for who he really is, because we finally have to admit that we didn't know as much as we thought we did. It's when life feels less like a problem we have to solve and more like an Algebra II test we forgot to study for.

When we realize we don't have the answers or the strength or the ability to get through something alone, when our resources are all gone, we look to God. In Genesis, as Moses and the children of Israel made their way to the Promised Land, they most clearly saw God's provision right in the middle of the Red Sea and, later, in the middle of the desert. Those were the places where he rescued them, gave them food to eat, water to drink, and shoes that did not wear out.

That's what happens in the middle of the dry and dusty places where things aren't always clear and problems seem to multiply and life feels overwhelming: we see God's provision and faithfulness. But if we spend our time feeling like our useful days are over and no one cares what we have to say anymore, then we miss out on some of the best things life has to offer. The thing we trust in the most will be the thing we hold onto the longest. So we have to decide, do we trust in ourselves and our fear of the future, or do we trust in God?

About a month ago, I was driving to watch Caroline play soccer. It was a weekday morning, and the sun had just started to come up over the clouds. I was in the car by myself and having a brutally honest conversation with God. There was a lot of "I don't know" and "I don't see how" and "I'm afraid of what's next." I prayed he would give me wisdom and direction and sustenance to get through this middle place of life where I've left being a young mother behind and moved on to something that feels decidedly less cute and fun. By the time I'd finished talking, I had tears rolling down my cheeks, and it was just a lot of emotion for a morning that was supposed to be focused on watching Caroline play soccer. But then I felt God say to me, *Trust me with this stage. Watch what I'll do. Trust me.* Then I looked out the window and saw the most subtle rainbow that had suddenly appeared in the clouds. In that moment, I knew that I was seen and loved and not forgotten here in the middle.

These are the years no one writes much about. There aren't as many pat answers, and there aren't as many cute stories. When I talk to other women my age, the commonality seems to be that we all feel stronger and smarter than we did in our twenties, but we also feel vulnerable and unsure as we try to figure out what's next. These are the years for both flailing and flying. We can feel good about using our hard-earned knowledge and our voices, but also unsure about where to use them. Both of those things can be true. We can feel sad that we have wrinkles around our mouths that make us look like we used to be chain smokers in a former life, and also eternally grateful that we have been able to grow old enough to have wrinkles. We can listen to James Taylor *and* Cardi B.

The middle place is the bright side when you choose to see it that way. Especially when you realize you're surrounded by love and light on all sides.

CHAPTER 4

THE BRIGHT SIDE OF
BEAUTY PRODUCTS AND AGING KIND OF GRACEFULLY

*Youth is a gift of nature, but age is a
work of art.*

—STANISLAW JERZY LEC

My friend Sophie sent me a text a while back with a link to a blog post about microneedling your face with one of those derm roller things that looks like a torture device, and then immediately applying Vitamin C serum while your skin is still open from all the little needles you just rolled over it. I realize this doesn't sound pleasant, but I immediately bought in because I am a sucker for a good beauty treatment.

I went to my bathroom cabinet and pulled out the derm roller I'd gotten when I went through a season of experimenting with the Rodan + Fields skincare line. I had abandoned R + F about a year earlier because their routine required approximately 462 steps both morning and night. Don't get me wrong; I want to look younger. I just don't want to spend two hours each day making it happen.

Anyway, I grabbed my derm roller and my Vitamin C serum, pulled my hair off my face, and went to town rolling and applying. Rolling and applying. By the time I was finished, my face burned like I was looking directly at the Ark of the Covenant in an Indiana Jones movie, but that only served to make me believe it was really working. I could literally feel my skin getting younger and smoother. And you know what? When I woke up the next morning, it really did look better. Is it just a placebo effect? *I don't care.*

When you find yourself in your mid-to-late forties, the mirror isn't always your friend. Most mornings I wake up feeling pretty good about myself, until I go to brush my teeth and see my grandmother staring back at me in the bathroom mirror. It's jarring. Where did those creases around my mouth come from? Did I become a marionette while I slept? Is that a new brown spot? Am I supposed to plant crops in those deep lines on my forehead? How long, O Lord, will I continue to have new age spots pop up on my face?

The answer? Forever. Because I grew up in the seventies and eighties when sunscreen meant you used Hawaiian Tropic SPF 2 to really make sure you were protected from all those harmful UV rays. That was my responsible alternative to baby oil. And listen, I spent those years with a golden glow that would make you weep with envy, but all those years of lying by the pool like it was my job have come back to haunt me. I have seen the sins of my past because they are laid out like a treasure map on my face. I also need to mention that my eyes are looking exception-ally droopy, and my eyebrows aren't helping the situation. I live in real fear that eventually, the whole top part of both my eyes will droop low enough to impair my eyesight, and then what?

All this to say, I am always on the search for the fountain of youth in the form of some lotion, cream, serum, or vitamin. This is the reason I only let myself go into Sephora on rare occasions: lest I leave with one of everything. I believe all the promises, all the hype, every single marketing ploy. Bonus points if a prod-uct has some sort of exotic ingredient such as Ashtanga berries grown on a hillside in a remote village in France and harvested by the monks at a neighboring monastery. I will hit "Buy Now" on Amazon so fast it will give you carpal tunnel to watch me. And then I try all my new products in the hope and the promise of a better tomorrow, until I take a good look in the mirror several weeks later and am left with the bitter disappointment and ago-nizing defeat that comes when I realize my face looks exactly the same as it did a month ago.

A while back, I bought not only a jar of something called Mizon All-in-One Snail Repair Cream, but some Mizon Snail Repair Intensive Anti-Wrinkle Formula. Because if you're going to go with products containing 92 percent snail mucus, then go big or go home. Plus, it was only about twenty dollars for both products, and what do I have to lose, other than possibly my breakfast when I think too much about putting snail mucus on my face?

The online instructions actually read, "The texture of snail cream is differented from other general creams which is very chewy like snail slime. To have more effective absorption, it is important to have tapping after applying."

First, I appreciate that they went with the word "differented," which isn't a real word at all. Even more, I wonder about my own discernment in choosing a product marketed by people who can't even use real words. What does that meeting look like? "Do we say it's one of a kind? No, let's go with 'differented.'"

Second, "which is very chewy like snail slime." Is "chewy" the right adjective here? Also, I just dry heaved.

As I went through the routine of washing my face and ex-foliating my face and moisturizing my face last night, I thought about the timeline of my skincare habits.

Birth to age twelve: I thought about my skin as much as I thought about the air I was breathing. It was flawless. Perfect.

It never even occurred to me to wear sunscreen, and parents in the 1970s were way too busy smoking cigarettes while mak-ing us bologna sandwiches on white Wonder bread slathered in

Miracle Whip to be bothered with the application of sunscreen. Ozone? Nobody even knew what that meant. Why are you talking to me about NASA and the space program?

I did go through a stage of wearing colored zinc oxide on my nose, but only because all the cool teenage lifeguards at the pool wore it. I didn't realize it served an actual purpose other than upping your cool factor. You know what else would have upped my cool factor? Not wearing my swim team one-piece racing suit to the pool every day.

I remember being excited to see some freckles show up on my nose because I felt this made me more like Ramona Quimby, Holly Hobbie, Laura Ingalls, or Kristy McNichol. Only now do I realize those freckles were basically a harbinger of early sun damage.

Age twelve to eighteen: The glory of puberty and hormones. This is when I learned that you have to wash your face every night. Especially if you enjoy slathering on Cover Girl foundation topped with a layer of face powder and Bonne Bell blush. Noxema was my favorite skin treatment because all that menthol and the white coating really made me feel like it was working. I was also a big fan of Sea Breeze astringent. I used it so much that I sometimes wonder if it's why my skin is dry to this very day.

My philosophy even back then was, if it's stinging like the fires of hell, then it must be working. I also used toothpaste on exceptionally bad breakouts. Thanks, *Seventeen Magazine*, for that tip.

I still didn't use sunscreen, unless you count baby oil. And I was a lifeguard almost every summer. I weep for my excellent life choices.

Age eighteen to twenty-four: It's hard to remember to take off your makeup when you stay out until 2:00 a.m. partying or studying.

Okay.

Just partying.

Yet my skin was resilient. It was like the Winona Ryder of skin. Just when I thought it couldn't possibly make a comeback, it did.

Age twenty-four to thirty-five: These were the years of a steady routine of basic skincare products. I discovered Cetaphil, which is still perfect for washing my face every night. I also learned that I had dry skin (Thanks, Sea Breeze!), and used some sort of rotation of Oil of Olay or Neutrogena moisturizer. Nothing fancy. Just whatever I happened to see at Walgreens or CVS that looked like it could do the job.

Other than an unfortunate, year-long period at age thirty-two after I gave birth to Caroline, during which I had post-pregnancy related melasma that was the exact shape of a mustache over my upper lip, it was a good time for my skin and me.

Yet I still never wore sunscreen unless I was specifically going to the pool or the beach. I'm not sure why it never occurred to me that the sun is, in fact, everywhere.

Age thirty-six to present day: It was right around the time Caroline turned four that she looked at me one morning and said, "Mama! I can see you brains on you forehead." It wasn't my brain she was seeing, it was worse. It was two deep wrinkles that seemed to appear overnight. I realized it was time to step up my skincare game.

Since that day, I have used countless products from countless different brands. I've tried things that are supposed to erase fine lines, reduce the appearance of dark spots, and basically perform miracles, all in the privacy of my bathroom. And the truth is, I'm sure most of it works okay. I don't know because I can't remember what my baseline face was at this point.

I do know that I spend more and more time every night before bed applying all manner of creams and lotions as I hum Cher's "If I Could Turn Back Time," and Perry yells out from the bedroom, "Are you ever coming to bed?" And I yell back, "You don't want to be married to some old hag. I'm trying to help you out." But I think the truth of aging is best summed up in the words of Truvy in *Steel Magnolias*: "Honey, time marches on, and eventually you realize it is marchin' across your face."

A friend told me the other day that she'd looked into getting Botox, but the question is, once you start all that, when do you stop? I don't really know the answer, but I'm sure it has to be the point at which your face becomes so frozen you can't drink through a straw or chew your food properly. When I watch the *Real Housewives of Beverly Hills* and one of them is sad, you can't even tell she's crying until she dabs at the tears under her eyes and her shoulders shake gently, because her face has ceased to move. I've been tempted to try fillers, but then I'll see a picture in *People* of some celebrity who now looks like a mutant cat due to bad fillers in her cheek and lip area. Essentially, these last few years feel more and more like I'm fighting at the Alamo and putting all my energy into making sure the landscaping looks nice. It's a battle you can't win.

Yet I continue to try new things, such as frankincense, Retin-A, vitamin E, and fasting and prayer. I slather on SPF 50 sunscreen even if I have no plans to be outside. I mean, I actually put snail mucus on my face. That's a bridge too far. I'm sure the snails agree, although I have been assured that no snails are harmed in the making of the snail cream. They get the mucus in a "differented" way that doesn't require a snail to die. And maybe the snails don't care because they look so young and vibrant and are as happy and carefree as a twenty-year-old girl who never remembers to wash off her makeup at night and thinks sunscreen is just for people who can't get a tan.

Anyway, here is a list of the beauty products I currently can't live without. Please note that the snail mucus didn't make the cut.

- *Rosehip oil*. It doesn't matter what brand you use. I am a firm believer in the power of rosehip oil. I use it morning and night after I wash my face, and it's just the right amount of moisturizer. I discovered this after I saw it had all five-star reviews on Amazon, which is basically like seeing a unicorn.

- *Nivea Crème made in Germany*. I realize this sounds fancy because of the specification "made in Germany." But my friend Jamie discovered that the first five ingredients of the Nivea Crème made in Germany are the same five ingredients found in La Mer, which is the holy grail of skincare. You can order Nivea Crème from Amazon and get a huge tub for the price of two Starbucks lattes. Or you can order La Mer from Neiman Marcus and eventually have to file for bankruptcy. However, your skin will glow as you walk the streets homeless in your bathrobe, so there's that.

- *Vitamin C serum*. There are a million brands of Vitamin C serum sold at various price points. It helps with fine lines and wrinkles, sun damage, and overall healing of the skin. It also helps with discoloration and brightening the skin.

Who doesn't need these things in their life? I see that hand in the back. Walk the aisle and get yourself saved with some Vitamin C.

- *Retinol.* Sister, get yourself a product with retinol. It's the gold standard for wrinkles and wrinkle prevention. If we have any hope of not ending up with faces that look like an elephant's knee, we need to incorporate retinol into our lives.

- *Sunscreen.* Get your life together and wear sunscreen every single day. You think you'll just be inside all day? *Lies.* If you have windows in your house, then you need to wear sunscreen. The sun is like the people who live in your phone and put ads on Instagram for things you casually mention in conversation: it's everywhere. And it's more than a little dangerous for your skin.

- *Water.* This is the cheapest, easiest skincare tip I can give you. Skin looks better when it's hydrated from the inside out. And I know water often tastes like sadness, but get some good ice and squeeze a lemon in it and go with God. You'll be glad you did.

I also have two bonus tips: Don't underestimate the youthful glow a good self-tanner can give you, and a silk pillowcase helps immensely with those face wrinkles that appear overnight. I've also been known to use surgical tape on my forehead during the night to keep my forehead pulled tight. I realize that's a little extra, but I come from a long line of vain women, and it's in my DNA. I know beauty is who you are on the inside, but I don't see my heart or my brain when I look in the mirror.

Truth be told, there are lots of benefits to getting older. I'm more secure in who I am. I'm not afraid to stand up for what I believe in. My perspective on life has shifted for the better, even if my eyelids have not.

The bright side is getting to grow old, because there isn't any kind of moisturizer that fixes the alternative.

CHAPTER 5

THE BRIGHT SIDE OF
BELIEVING IN
EVER AFTER

Marriage is kind of like being a member of a street gang. You pretty much have to die to get out easily.

—PERRY SHANKLE

I recently started watching Marie Kondo's Netflix show, *Tidying Up*. In case you have been living in a cave that's probably very cluttered, Marie Kondo is the author of a hugely successful book titled *The Life-Changing Magic of Tidying Up*. I never read the book because I heard through the grapevine that she suggests saying thank you to your old clothing before you give it away, and the only time I tend to talk to my clothing is when I splurge on a gorgeous sweater from Anthropologie and greet it with "Hello, Lover," as I pull it out of the shopping bag.

The reason I'm watching her show at all is solely because it premiered in early January, and there is never a time when I am more optimistic about being my best self than once the Christmas tree comes down. I am going to eat cleaner, exercise more often, read the entire Bible in a year, and organize the whole house by throwing out all the things we don't need or use. I may even buy some baskets. This year, I actually switched out the hangers in my closet from plastic to those velvet huggable hangers, which was a total game changer, by the way.

Thankfully, this foray into self-improvement generally doesn't make it past January 15 because, frankly, it's exhausting, and I set myself up for failure by committing to way too much for a person whose greatest accomplishment in the month of December, by her own admission, was re-watching all five seasons of *Friday Night Lights*.

Anyway, one of Marie Kondo's premises for how to clean

out your home is to evaluate your things and ask yourself if it "sparks joy." Do I love these jeans? Do I feel good in this sweater? Does it bring me joy? First, let me say, that's a lot of pressure to put on a pair of leggings from Old Navy. Second, I immediately decided to assess my own closet using this method. Here's what I discovered: I like my stuff. Do I wear all of it? No. But I might. What if one day I wake up and decide that the striped sweater I haven't worn in five years is exactly the thing I want to wear today? Not to mention that if I got rid of something anytime it didn't bring me joy, I wouldn't have managed to stay married for twenty-two years. Just because something doesn't bring you joy today doesn't mean it won't bring you joy tomorrow. And that is maybe the best commentary on marriage that I can offer. Thank you, Marie Kondo, for helping me sum that up.

I'm not the first person to say that marriage isn't easy, and that's because marriage isn't easy. You take two people with different personalities, temperaments, ideas of what constitutes an ideal temperature and backgrounds, and then put them not only in the same house, but in the same bed. Then you add in all the stressful parts of life, such as finances, raising kids, how to celebrate holidays and cleaning up the dog's throw-up, and you have a recipe for some tension. This is why the Cinderella story ends with her and the prince riding away from the castle in a glass carriage after the wedding. The sequel would have revealed that Prince Charming snores too loud and that Cinderella goes to bed with surgical tape on her forehead to help with her wrinkles in a sorority T-shirt she's owned since her freshman year of college. No one is writing a fairy tale about that.

The other day, I started thinking about love songs that made me feel all swoony and in love with the idea of love I had when I was younger. I'm going to list a few here with some additions to make them line up better with the reality of love after twenty-plus years of marriage.

"Waiting for a Girl Like You" *to get ready for the last thirty minutes. I'm about to leave for church without you.* (Foreigner)

"Hard to Say I'm Sorry" *because I know that you're wrong and I'm right.* (Chicago)

"Love Me Tomorrow" *since tonight, I just want to read my* People *magazine and scroll through Instagram.* (Chicago)

"All Out of Love" *because you left me alone with your mother for thirty minutes.* (Air Supply)

"Never Gonna Let You Go" *hunting this weekend because I've had to manage these kids by myself all week long.* (Sérgio Mendes)

"Let's Get It On" *but I'm going to leave my socks on because I'm freezing.* (Marvin Gaye)

"I Don't Want to Miss a Thing" *except for how you can't pick your dirty socks up off the floor and put them in the laundry hamper.* (Aerosmith)

"Have I Told You Lately" *that I hate when you talk on your cell phone when we're in the car together.* (Van Morrison)

"Just the Way You Are" *except we're going to need to throw out that blue shirt you always wear.* (Billy Joel)

"I Just Called to Say I Love You" *and don't forget to pick up dog food on the way home.* (Stevie Wonder)

"The Way You Look Tonight" *is a far cry from how you looked on our wedding day. Nice sweatpants and Korean sheet face mask.* (Harry Connick, Jr.)

Last summer, Caroline and I had a nightly movie marathon during which we watched a variety of movies from my teen years—also known as the eighties—when teen angst was a regular player at the cinema. Of course, we ended up watching *Pretty in Pink*, which, if a movie defined my teen years, that is the one. I bet I saw it a hundred times between 1986 and 1991. I owned the soundtrack on a cassette tape that I listened to until the cassette player in my Honda CRX ate it, and no amount of twisting those little plastic holes with a pencil was going to fix it. I always cheered and cried when Andie ended up with Blane at the end of the movie. That was true love. That was what I wanted someday.

Except that when I watched it last summer, my older self couldn't have disagreed more. Blane has zero backbone. He lets his friend, Steff, totally bully him into breaking his prom date with Andie and then can't own up to it, even when she confronts him in the hallway at school and yells, "WHAT ABOUT PROM, BLANE? WHAT ABOUT PROM?" Blane is the guy who eventually gets arrested for insider trading because Steff told him it was a can't-miss opportunity and he was dumb enough to listen. It doesn't matter that he had some very fancy DOS computer skills back in 1986; do not choose Blane. If anything, choose Duckie. He's the eccentric guy who turns out to be the one everyone at the ten-year reunion wishes they'd noticed in high school because he's now wildly successful and just a genuinely good guy who was mocked by the Blanes and Steffs of the world because he liked a bolo tie and rode his bike to school.

And here's the thing my younger, swoony self couldn't have known: real, lasting, we-are-in-this-for-better-or-for-worse love is so much better than the fairy tale or a guy named Blane who wears chambray shirts. It's messier and more complicated at times, yes, but it's deep and true and worth the fight to get to the other side. You can look back at a shared history and know that you have forged something stronger than you could have imagined. You are two imperfect people who have found a way to make a life together, and that in and of itself is a living miracle.

* ✳ *

A few years ago, Perry went on a ten-day hunting trip to Colorado with a friend. He came home with both a mule deer and an elk. Guess who got a new set of antlers in her living room and enough meat in the freezer to last through at least three *Little House on the Prairie*-style winters? This girl.

When he left for the trip, I basically prayed that nothing would happen while he was gone. I mean, yes, I wanted him to have safe travel and a good hunt and all that, but I also wanted life around here to be boring and uneventful. I didn't want to hear any weird sounds in the night or have the house alarm go off or have my car break down or a pipe burst in the wall. Essentially, I didn't want to have to be a big girl and handle any of the things that fall under his jurisdiction while he was out of town. Which is basically anything that requires maintenance and/or figuring out weird sounds in the middle of the night.

All was going well until one night, when I noticed that our dogs, Piper and Mabel, were suddenly obsessed with the fireplace. They are trained hunting dogs, and their noses are designed to track animals, so I found this new fascination with the fireplace slightly concerning. Vermin in the vicinity of our home are solely under Perry's category of expertise. My tendency is to deal with vermin the way normal people do, which is to say I put a For Sale sign in the front yard and move.

For days, every time Piper and Mabel came in the house, they went immediately to the fireplace and proceeded to growl at each other, which was a sure sign there was something interesting there that neither wanted to share with her sister.

But then, probably due to my many prayers to this end, they seemed to lose interest in the fireplace, and I decided maybe they'd both just been intrigued by the scent of my new lavender-eucalyptus candle, because hunting dogs are known to go wild for a good candle, am I right? So I kind of forgot about it, and Perry got home from his trip with his mule deer and his elk, and life seemed to be back to normal, but with a thousand pounds of meat in our freezer and some new antlers on display.

However, a few days later, Piper and Mabel both became intensely focused on the fireplace again, so I casually said to Perry, "That's so weird. They did that while you were gone, too. I wonder what's going on?"

"Did you open the damper to see if there was anything up there?" he asked.

Yes. Sure, I did. Right after I lit myself on fire.

We have been married for over twenty years. I barely have the courage to open the damper to make a fire in the fireplace on a cold night when he's out of town, so in what world am I going to open it to investigate something clearly dark and sinister lurking about? I may not have seen the movie It, Jenny, but I know what clowns are.

Perry immediately grabbed his flashlight and decided to check it out. He was joined by trusty Piper, because Mabel happened to be outside eating her dinner and was unaware of the potential excitement at hand. It was precisely two minutes later that he quietly and calmly said, *"OH, SH*%!"* as he found himself staring eye-to-eye with a large raccoon, which had made itself at home in our chimney. Because I am always calm and cool in a crisis, I yelled, "WHAT IS YOUR PLAN? BECAUSE I AM LITERALLY GOING TO LOSE MY MIND IF A RACCOON ENDS UP IN MY LIVING ROOM!"

This is why it is fortunate that these types of situations fall under Perry's particular set of skills. In the time it took me to freak the freak out, he had closed the damper and cut off the raccoon's potential entry into our domicile. After that near-life-altering crisis was averted, I asked him what he would have done had the raccoon actually jumped out of the fireplace, to which he replied, "I figured the dogs could have taken him."

Isn't that a cheery thought? Who doesn't want to think about how two dogs attacking a raccoon could alter the state of your living area? How does one feng shui oneself back to normalcy after that? Not even Marie Kondo could tidy that up.

The answer is, you'd have to burn the place to the ground.

The next morning, Perry climbed up on the roof and looked down the chimney to make sure the raccoon had vacated the premises before securing the top of the chimney with a metal grate so the raccoon would have to find a new place to crash. But Piper still remembers what was almost the most exciting night of her life and is convinced she'll be able to meet up with that raccoon again if she just tries hard enough.

Meanwhile, I have my suspicions that the raccoon is parading around up on our roof, celebrating how he came face-to-face with a man wearing gingerbread print pajama bottoms and lived to tell about it. And Mabel watches Piper continue to obsess over the raccoon with a little bit of pity and disdain.

She naturally wrote a haiku about it:

> I sensed dirty paws
> trash panda lurking about
> You're not welcome here

And Piper wrote a poem, too:

PLS COME BCK. I WOOD LIKE TO FITE U.

Ultimately, I realized that "raccoon in the chimney" is a very real reason I'm glad to be married to Perry. Sometimes a knight in shining armor looks a lot like being the one who's brave enough to open the damper and investigate.

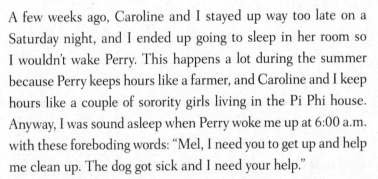

A few weeks ago, Caroline and I stayed up way too late on a Saturday night, and I ended up going to sleep in her room so I wouldn't wake Perry. This happens a lot during the summer because Perry keeps hours like a farmer, and Caroline and I keep hours like a couple of sorority girls living in the Pi Phi house. Anyway, I was sound asleep when Perry woke me up at 6:00 a.m. with these foreboding words: "Mel, I need you to get up and help me clean up. The dog got sick and I need your help."

I stumbled out of bed and began to follow him back to our bedroom when he turned to me, grabbed my shoulders, and gravely said, "You need to prepare yourself for what you're about to see. You also need to change out of those flowy pants." Nothing says "level ten catastrophe" like the need to change out of your flowy pants. By this time, I could smell the awfulness emanating throughout the house, so I knew this was serious. Let me also say that a week before this, our air conditioner started leaking through the bathroom ceiling at 3:30 a.m., and I thought that was probably the worst house catastrophe we would deal with this summer. How I wish I could go back to being the sweet, naïve girl who believed that to be true.

Side note: When our air conditioner was leaking through the bathroom ceiling at 3:30 a.m., you better believe I absolutely woke Perry up to deal with it. He climbed up in the attic to begin the process of finding the problem, which turned out to be a clogged drain that was causing condensation to accumulate and overflow into the ceiling. He then told me to put on a head-lamp and climb up in the attic so he could show me how to fix it in case it ever happened again. Nothing really overstates his confidence and belief in my alleged abilities like when he shows me how to do a home repair by myself next time, because that is never going to happen. That's why you have a husband. Or an emergency on-call A/C repair service you can summon.

But back to the dog situation. I'm here to tell you that what I encountered as I walked through our bedroom door was like standing on the threshold of hell. One time, when Caroline was about six months old, I was concerned about her lack of bowel movements and made the rookie mistake of feeding her a jar of baby food prunes and then putting her in her Johnny-Jump-Up about an hour later. That's when I learned poop can fly.

This was worse than that.

Perry pointed me toward the box of latex gloves he'd already gotten from the backhouse, when he still believed the clean-up was a one-person job, and then handed me my own roll of paper towels and disinfectant. Here's what you never want to think about at 6:00 a.m. on a Sunday or—well, ever. How does a dog manage to get poop that high up on the wall? You know when people refer to something as a s*&% show? This was a literal s*&% show. I honestly wondered if we could just drag the garden hose through the window and spray everything down. Or if we should just move to a new home and ask the city to condemn this one.

It was on the dust ruffle; it was on the gift wrap storage container that I keep under the bed; it was a trail that led to our shower and throughout our bathroom. Mercifully, she spared our closet. We cleaned and wiped and sprayed and dry-heaved for the next forty-five minutes. Caroline woke up from the smell and began to open up every window in the entire house, light every candle we own, and turn all the fans and vents on high. Meanwhile, Piper stared at us through the back door like, "What's the deal? Where's my breakfast?" as if she had totally forgotten this was all her fault.

As we were making sure every last inch of our bedroom and bathroom were scrubbed clean, I finally asked Perry what exactly happened and when he realized Piper was sick. He said he woke up to something bumping and shaking the bed, and that's when the smell hit him. He found Piper in the bathroom getting sick and got her outside, then discovered our other dog, Mabel, hiding under the bed. She wanted no part of whatever was going on with her sister and ran for cover. And you know, she wrote a haiku about it while she was hiding out:

> Hiding from the stench
> Told her she shouldn't eat that
> Plus, she didn't share

Needless to say, Piper—or any of us, for that matter—didn't feel much like eating the rest of the day. The lesson I learned is that sometimes marriage is a literal s*$% show (I believe that's in the Bible), and also, there is no such thing as too much bleach. Finally, this is a scenario a girl can never imagine on her wedding day.

* * *

A while back, I read a novel called *The Husband's Secret* by Liane Moriarty. Here's a simplified version of the plot: A husband writes a letter to his wife, containing a secret, which is to be opened in the event of his death. However, she stumbles across the letter while he is out of town on a business trip and has to decide whether or not to read it, even though her husband is still very much alive. The novel itself is entertaining, but I contend that anyone who has been married for any length of time knows this is a bad premise for a book because, unless you are a saint, that letter would be ripped open and read before you even made it down the attic steps. I verified this when I mentioned the plot of the book to Perry one night over dinner and asked him what he would do if he found a letter like that from me. He confirmed he would open it, and he's usually a much better person than I am. Although he did say, in his defense, that I've been dead to him several times throughout our two decades of marriage. I know what you're thinking, and yes, I married the last of the sweet-talkers.

Then, the other day, I was reading one of those articles about funny things kids say, instead of writing this book like I'm supposed to be doing, and one of the kids was asked this question: "How can a stranger tell if two people are married?" He answered, "I guess you just see if they're yelling at the same kids."

Yes. That about sums it up.

Because even though we walk down that long, dramatic aisle wearing a gorgeous white gown with stars in our eyes like Kate Middleton, the reality soon sinks in that sometimes marriage is hard. So here is what I will tell you: choose wisely, young Jedi.

(Am I the Yoda of marriage? Apparently so.)

When you are dating, keep your eyes open. When he shows you things about who he is, both good and bad, believe them. Watch how he treats others, see how he lives out his faith, determine if he's a man of character and integrity. Does he make you laugh? Does he challenge you? Does he inspire you to be a better person? Is there more to the relationship than the fact that you can't keep your hands off each other? Is he a good friend? Can you trust him? Does he offer grace when you make a mistake? Attraction is important, but his character is crucial. Because these are the things that remain when the band quits playing and you leave your lovely wedding reception under a bridge of your friends holding sparklers and blowing bubbles. And if there is a point when, even after you are engaged and the cocktail shrimp is already on ice at your reception, you decide he isn't the person you want to marry, don't be afraid to call off the wedding. I believe 99.9 percent of parents would rather lose their deposit on a wedding cake than see their child make the mistake of marrying the wrong person.

Marriage is when the relationship settles into real life, and it doesn't fix anything. Grocery shopping and children and assembling furniture, budgeting money and navigating each other's families and cleaning up when the dog poops in your bedroom. Depending on the day, all of these can be equally difficult tasks.

There was one morning when I got mad at Perry for asking me if we were out of raw sugar because it felt like more of an accusation than a question. I stirred my coffee angrily while thinking, *I don't need you to just raw sugar all over me at 8:00 in the morning.* It's at this point that you begin to understand that marriage is maybe not what you thought it would be, and your husband is not who you thought he'd be, and additionally, you are not who you thought you'd be. You realize that maybe your husband is more turned on when you actually make the time to take your car to get the tires rotated and balanced than he is by seeing you in lingerie. And those glossy 8 x 10 photos from the wedding day that sit framed on the bookshelves are the only thing that remain of all our dreams of being so different from all the other married couples who have gone before us because marriage, even in the very best of circumstances, requires maintenance and work and compromise and dying to yourself over and over again.

Perry and I have been married enough years that we argue about the thermostat and what show that actor from *Schitt's Creek* was on fifteen years ago. We have seen the better and the worse, the richer and the poorer, the sickness and the health. Our life together is a timeline which, if charted on graph paper, would show some high highs and some low lows. It hasn't always been easy, and there have been days or even years when we weren't sure how we were going to make it through, but we've covered it in a lot of prayer, asking God to give us the strength and wisdom and gentleness and patience we need to make it through another day. And then another year. And for the rest of our lives. Because that's the goal: the ever after that is sometimes happily and sometimes begrudgingly, but is the destination we all hope for when we say those vows in front of our friends and family. Sometimes you have to look at any relationship and ask yourself, "Is there more good here than bad?" and then decide that the good is worth it.

It's not always that a marriage has problems as much as two people with problems got married. We bring all of our stuff and all of our baggage, and sometimes it's not going to look pretty because we are being refined in the process of becoming one. In fact, sometimes it's going to feel like the fight of our lives. Take it from Gideon, who learned what it means to fight for what really matters.

In Judges 6, there is a story about the Israelites being oppressed by the Midianites. They are living in fear and losing everything they valued. But then an angel appears to a man named Gideon.

> When the angel of the LORD appeared to Gideon, he said, "The LORD is with you, mighty warrior."
>
> "Pardon me, my lord," Gideon replied, "but if the LORD is with us, why has all this happened to us? Where are all his wonders that our ancestors told us about when they said, 'Did not the LORD bring us up out of Egypt?' But now the LORD has abandoned us and given us into the hand of Midian."
>
> The LORD turned to him and said, "Go in the strength you have and save Israel out of Midian's hand. Am I not sending you?"
>
> "Pardon me, my lord," Gideon replied, "but how can I save Israel? My clan is the weakest in Manasseh, and I am the least in my family."
>
> The LORD answered, "I will be with you, and you will strike down all the Midianites, leaving none alive." (Judges 6:12–16)

Marriage—and even more than that, life—is going to come with struggles and problems. No matter how great two people are, life is hard, and there will be temptations and failures and disappointments and hurt feelings and broken dreams. There will be times we feel like God has let us down or this is more than we signed on for. But this is what I notice as the angel speaks to Gideon—he tells him, "Go in the strength you have." Gideon responds with all the reasons the strength he has isn't enough, and that's when God says, "I will be with you."

God is with us. Always. In our marriages. In our lives. In the good days and the bad days. He is the most real and most true love of our lives, and anything in life worth doing can't be done in our own strength. It is God who equips us, gives us the strength we need, and gives us the wisdom and the grace and all those fruits of the Spirit that make a marriage work—those things that are hard to find when someone insists on leaving their dirty towel on the bathroom floor and their Band-Aid wrappers on the kitchen counter. When the hard days come, go in the strength you have and trust that God is meeting you exactly in that place to give you everything else you need.

Also, it helps to remember that there was a time when we were *dying* for these men to be our husbands. We cried *real tears* to our girlfriends about how much we loved them and agonized over when they'd finally propose. It's good to remember those days. Especially on the days when you realize he ate the left-overs you planned to serve for dinner for his lunch, then asks you, "What's for dinner?"

Life is serious. There are bills to pay and problems to solve and kids to potty train. But don't forget to laugh because, let's face it, sometimes life is absurd, and I think we do better when we acknowledge that. I've always said Perry's saving grace is that I still think he's hilarious. Not every day, necessarily, but often enough that I'm still glad he's the one who comes home to me every day. Make each other laugh. Bonus points if you can do it and put an end to a stupid fight you were having a minute earlier. We were in Nashville a couple of years ago with some friends, and we were talking about the importance of laughter in a marriage when Perry said, "There are two things that are important in a marriage. Laughter is one and communication isn't the other."

On that note, do not underestimate the importance of sex.

Don't forget to carve out time to spend together as a couple. Those kids who take up every minute of your time will be gone one day, and you don't want to look across the table at a spouse who's become a stranger while you were busy driving carpool and trying to make cupcakes that look like melting snowmen, which you saw on Pinterest. If you want your husband to see you as more than a mom, then you need to show him a side of you that isn't just a mom. Try to talk about things you used to talk about, and not just whether or not the kids need to be gluten-free or who's driving to soccer practice. Take time to sit on the couch together at the end of the day and talk when you can. Dream together and laugh together, because it helps you remember why you fell in love all those years ago. Don't neglect the relationship that brought you the kids in the first place. Ultimately, a healthy marriage is the best gift you can give your children. It's a legacy they won't even know to appreciate until they're grown, but it shapes every part of their lives. Whenever Perry and I are feeling disconnected, it's usually because we've let too many days go by without spending quality time together. It's always worth the effort and usually serves as a reset button.

Remember, too, to give yourself grace. You're going to burn dinner, forget to pick up the dry cleaning, and have PMS. You're going to get mad when someone asks you about raw sugar. None of us are June Cleaver; we are doing the best we can. At the end of the day, we have succeeded if our families feel loved and safe. Some days, it's a victory that you kept everyone alive and mostly fed for the day.

And then—this is a big one—forgive each other. One of the biggest realizations I've come to over the years is that Perry is never intentionally trying to hurt me. He may say or do something insensitive, but he never purposely wants to anger me. I know this because he now sometimes prefaces a hard statement with, "I'm trying to find a way to say this that won't make you mad." He gets it right about 75 percent of the time.

Sometimes I hear about couples who are getting divorced after thirty-five years of marriage, and I always kind of feel like, "What's the point?" It seems like, if you've made it that long, you can stick with it for the duration. But it's also a sobering reminder that marriage is a constant work in progress. We never reach a finish line and get to declare that we have arrived and are victorious. It's a daily promise to compromise and die to our own selfish desires, to remember we live with another human who may drive us crazy because he only uses half a paper towel and leaves the other half on the counter, but that we vowed to love him for better or for worse until death do us part. Sometimes the key to a successful marriage is working at it even when we don't feel like it. It's loving our spouses when they seem unlovable and remembering that we might not be a picnic to live with either on some days. Although this isn't the case for me. I'm sure Perry would agree if you asked him, but he isn't available for questions right now.

Embrace reality and open your arms wide to the *real* him, the *real* you, and *real* marriage, and trust God to meet you there. Because here's the thing: there is a place where work and hope and faith all collide, and it's called marriage.

It's wonderful.

And frustrating.

On the bright side, happily ever after is, at best, a myth. But the reality can be good, too. If nothing else, you'll always have someone to check your fireplace for raccoons.

CHAPTER 6

THE BRIGHT SIDE OF
STAYING MOSTLY SANE WHILE RAISING KIDS

Never lend your car to anyone to whom you have given birth.

—ERMA BOMBECK

When I found out I was pregnant for the first time, I lay awake that night wondering, *Do I know how to be a good mom?* And then three weeks later, I lay on a cold, sterile table as my doctor searched in vain for the heartbeat of a baby who had briefly been there and was now gone. Tears rolled down my face as I walked out of his office, grieving for a baby who was suddenly a memory instead of a reality. I was devastated and heartbroken, but what I didn't know that day was that I had just arrived at the threshold of what it means to be a good mom. Good moms love so deeply that our hearts are never the same.

A little less than two years later, I held Caroline in my arms. Miraculously, the hospital staff just let us load her into our car, checking only to make sure we had a properly installed car seat, and we took her home. I had no idea what I was doing, but I had skimmed several parenting books. Surely they would help me be a good mom as I figured out feeding schedules and how to cut teeny-tiny, razor-sharp baby fingernails, and—oh my gosh— what do I do with this umbilical cord stump?

Now that I'm almost sixteen years down this motherhood road, I've realized that being a good mom doesn't mean being a perfect mom. A perfect mom puts sand in a plastic box so her toddler can have a meaningful sensory experience and doesn't care about the mess. A perfect mom plays board games for hours on end, makes hot chocolate with organic milk and candy cane stir sticks, and serves chicken nuggets made only from chickens who were allowed to roam free in sunlit barns. She never loses her patience, never checks her text messages while her child is around, and is the president of the parent/teacher association while managing a Fortune 500 company, after which she returns home at night to prepare a delicious, nutritious meal for her family.

In short, the perfect mom doesn't exist. And if she did, we would all hate her.

The perfect mom is a unicorn, mythical at best. But a good mom is the velveteen rabbit, a little worn from use. And while I'm not confident in a lot of areas of my life, I'm confident I'm a good mom, because what ultimately makes a good mom is showing up. I've held back hair as she's thrown up over the toilet (and, I regret to say, all over me). I've wiped her bottom and her feverish forehead. I've stayed in the school parking lot long after she's walked through the school doors, praying and hoping that today would be a better day. I've sat in the rain, the cold, and the heat that rivals the surface of the sun to watch her play soccer. I've cried when she's overwhelmed by joy, and I've cried when disappointments have her down. I've yelled too much, lost my patience, and seen how many mornings I can get by with Frosted Flakes for breakfast. I've driven more carpools than I can count, attended Taylor Swift concerts, and spent many weekend nights with my house full of tween girls with high-pitched squeals who think cleaning up after themselves means putting half-empty soda cans under the bed. I've looked at my phone too often, set the clock ahead an hour so I could tell her it was time for bed, and pretended to have an upset stomach just so I could have a few minutes alone in the bathroom.

But I have no doubt she knows she is deeply loved, because I have faithfully shown up for the job for the last sixteen years.

It hasn't been perfect, it hasn't always been pretty, and nobody is likely to turn our story into an award-winning movie. Being a good mom doesn't really make the highlight reel because there is very little glamour in packing another peanut butter and jelly sandwich for lunch. It's just about being faithful with what has been entrusted to you for such a short time that I could sob thinking about it. It's loving hard, laughing loud, crying when you are at your breaking point, hugging them tight, and having a good bakery on speed dial, because there isn't any way you are going to be able to make a birthday cake like the ones the mythical perfect moms post on Pinterest. It's messy, loud, beautiful, mundane, exhilarating, and gut-wrenching all at the same time.

I wouldn't trade it for anything in the world.

* * *

The other day, I saw a woman wearing a shirt that read, "Oops! I forgot to have children!" across the front, and I kind of wanted to run up and give her a hug while whispering, "You, madam, are my spirit animal." Except that would be weird on a lot of levels, so I buried the impulse.

I didn't forget to have children. I just had a child. One child. And lean in closer while I make this confession: Perry and I made that decision on purpose.

It's not really what I'd planned for myself when I was younger and daydreamed about my future family. In fact, I went through a phase in the mid-eighties when I imagined myself with five children that I would name Mandy, Randy, Candy, Sandy, and Andy. And now you're probably thinking it all worked out for the best that I ended up having only one.

I certainly never envisioned myself being any kind of spokesperson for the only-child crowd, but over my last eleven years as a blogger, the question I get the most is whether or not I have regrets that we never gave Caroline a sibling. That's a hard question, because the number of kids you and your husband decide to have is an extremely personal decision, although you wouldn't necessarily know that by all the complete strangers who feel free to regularly ask, "So, when are you going to have another one?" or, "Don't you worry about what will happen to her when you die and she's left all alone in the world?" People are so great. And by this, I mean they can be extremely insensitive and feel like they have the right to get in your business even if you just met them on an airplane or in line at Starbucks.

When Caroline was about to start kindergarten, I began to think I wanted another child. I shared my feelings with Perry, and he really didn't agree with my assessment of the state of our family. We both agreed we would pray about it and see where we landed. But I was plagued by questions such as, *What happens if we screw her up and end up as two old people who have to spend holidays with just the dog?* I'd google articles about only children, reassuring myself that they often ended up being higher achievers, leaders, and, most importantly, not automatically in therapy from not having a sibling. But then I'd see a picture of Caroline as a squishy toddler and think back nostalgically on those days and wonder if I wanted to do it all over again. Would I regret not doing it again? Would she be okay without a brother or a sister?

Ultimately, I began to realize that while some of my concerns were legitimate, the majority of them were based on my perception of what a family was supposed to look like. It's the American ideal, right? Two cars in the garage, at least two kids (preferably a boy and a girl), and a chicken in every pot. I think maybe that was some politician's campaign slogan in the 1950s. However, when I blocked out the external noise, the well-meaning questions, and my own insecurities about people making me feel like I was less of a mom for having just one child, and I focused instead on what was really best for our family, I felt completely secure in our decision to have one child. As I continued to pray about it, I knew in my heart that God was telling me our family was complete.

Ultimately, I need to do what works best for me. I need to realize that someone else's decision to have seven kids has no bearing on my decision to have one, and vice versa. I believe that rather than a selfish decision, having an only child was accepting what we were emotionally, physically, and financially prepared for. It really dawned on me one day when Caroline and I visited the home of one of her kindergarten classmates, who happened to be the youngest of four kids. As that mom and I sat and attempted to visit, there was a constant stream of yelling, jumping, crashing noises, and shrieks as what seemed to be a pack of wild children ran in and out of the house. This mom wasn't fazed by it in the least; she kept up her end of the conversation and never skipped a beat. It was like she was having high tea at a fancy resort, and I was a frightened dog at a fireworks show.

Later that week, when I saw my fellow moms chasing toddlers all around the neighborhood pool, I realized I had entirely lost my nostalgia for those days and felt nothing but the relief of a prisoner on parole to be able to just sit and watch my independent big kid jump off the diving board. I didn't miss the days of praying that swim diapers wouldn't explode or having a little person do that thing where they make their whole body go stiff and you have to carry them out of a public place like they're a fifty-pound log who's kicking and screaming.

Perry and I have each had plenty of time to cultivate our own unique relationship with Caroline because she has all of our focus—for better or for worse, in her opinion, depending on the day. It also helps that Caroline is completely content with her only-child status. However, we have worked hard to make sure she doesn't live up to the stereotype of the spoiled only child. Yes, she probably gets a few more gifts at Christmas because she's the only one we have to buy gifts for, but we have raised her to have character, integrity, and a heart that focuses on those around her. There are plenty of kids with siblings who turn out entitled and selfish, because the character of children is ultimately determined by what is instilled in them by their parents, not by how many brothers or sisters they have. We have worked hard to make sure Caroline treats the world around her with kindness and respect, and in some ways, I think being an only child has helped her focus on her friendships even more because her friends are the closest thing to family she has outside of us.

These days, I'm completely at peace with having an only child unless I've watched an episode of *Parenthood* on Netflix. How fulfilled can you be in life if you aren't a Braverman who regularly dines outdoors under twinkly lights with your grown siblings? But as I watch the woman Caroline is becoming, I believe all the more that our decision was the right one for our family because it was what God called us to be. We are a little band of three, and that has been the perfect fit for all of us.

And best of all, I will never have the need to own a minivan. Although now that they have those fancy doors that open and close on their own, maybe I'm a little bit sad about that.

ON THE BRIGHT SIDE

I don't know the secret to raising kids to become productive members of society who won't shame your family name. There is no one right way to raise kids, and there is no 100 percent foolproof method that will determine the outcome. We've made decisions for our family that will look much different from the decisions others make. That doesn't mean any of us are wrong; it just means we have to trust God with where he leads us, even when that looks different from our own or someone else's expectations. The point of any call from God is to teach us to depend on him, and nothing does that quite like parenthood. We don't have all the answers. Most days we don't even know most of the questions. I keep saying that having a teenager is like being required to take a pop quiz every single day and—SURPRISE!—there's a bonus essay question you have to answer at 10:30 p.m. every night after your second glass of wine. You are constantly humbled in new and interesting ways. You never knew that someone could roll their eyes completely out of their head as you show off the fact that you can rap along with Cardi B.

So much has been said and written about how to change the world, but I believe the biggest opportunity we have is to raise the next generation. The legacy of family is the most important thing we leave behind. I believe the children are our future, teach them well and let them lead the way, just like Whitney told us all those years ago, God rest her soul.

But here's what I've learned along the way. Be honest with your kids. Because, I promise you, they're going to be honest with you, especially once they are teenagers. I bought a new pair of sunglasses the other day and wore them for the first time in front of my best friend, Gulley. She raved about them, told me how cute I looked in them, and even said she wanted to get a pair just like them. With that confidence boost, I wore them to pick up Caroline from school. She got in the car, took one look at me, and said, "Mom, no. You look like Edna from *The Incredibles*." Which made me want to say, *Remember that time when you were four and I told you I could totally tell your drawing was of a princess with a butterfly crown? I lied.*

Here's the thing: kids are smart. It doesn't take them long to figure out when you're being honest and when you're not. Kids see hypocrisy a mile away, and if they don't see character and integrity modeled in your actions, then they have no motivation to do so in their own lives.

Sometimes they need us to be their coach and not just a cheerleader. We're the ones who help them figure out life. When we tell them everything they do is great, we can kill their motivation to work hard, and it can diminish their trust in us because kids aren't dumb. They know when they've done well and when they haven't. When we acknowledge they didn't do well, we're telling them that we understand their disappointment, and they know they can count on us to tell them the truth, which means our praise actually means something.

The cold, hard truth is that not everyone wins, not everyone makes the talent show, and, later in life, not everyone gets accepted to their first college choice or gets the job. We have to teach them what it means to fail and try again. We have to equip them for what lies ahead. We have to instill resilience if we expect them to amount to anything.

Let's encourage them, challenge them, and give them an internal drive to succeed by teaching them the value of perseverance, diligence, and responsibility. Those things will have a much bigger impact on their lives and future success than making an A on a test or winning a game.

I've also learned that I sometimes want to parent out of fear, and that's not good for any of us. I know. You just felt more afraid when you read that. I know that because I feel a little afraid writing it. We want to wrap our kids in bubble wrap so nothing can hurt them, ever. But when we look back at our own lives, isn't it the things that hurt us most that also did the most to shape us? We are a generation of parents who would put our kids in one enormous bike helmet if we could. But if we're always scared, then we're going to raise kids who are scared. And you know what scared kids *don't* do? Grow up to be people who impact their world.

I get it. There are so many concerns and worries. Organic versus non-organic; car seats, booster seats, or full five-point harness seats; private school, public school, or homeschool; gluten or no gluten; free-range chicken or Kentucky Fried? There is so much pressure and there are so many conflicting voices and there are so many ways we can get it wrong without even meaning to. In the 1970s, moms were considered a success if they cracked the car window while they smoked their Virginia Slims and drove around with us all rolling around in the back seat. Now we are expected to make childhood magical and special at every turn.

The constant wondering if you're doing enough only leads to constant parental guilt. Kids sense that business within a hundred-mile radius and will work you over like a rented circus monkey. The what-ifs will make you want to stay in bed, and the thing about forecasting worst-case scenarios is that we can never accurately imagine the mercy and grace God will give us for whatever may come. Let's teach our kids to be brave, even if that means we sometimes have to pretend to be less scared than we really are as we watch them learn to fly.

About a month ago, Caroline asked me if I'd buy her a pair of royal blue Crocs to wear before and after her soccer games. Yes, Crocs. You heard me. Soccer players have brought Crocs back to the forefront of society. So I ordered a pair from Amazon Prime and when they arrived on our porch about two minutes later, she immediately took them out of the package and adorned them with various Jibbitz, such as a soccer ball, a number six, a lightning bolt, and Lightning McQueen. The Lightning McQueen was an unexpected touch. But what happened later was even more unexpected.

I walked into her bathroom late one night doing that thing where you make the rounds before you go to bed in an attempt to rein in some of the clutter and mess and dirty socks so that you won't have to face it all in the morning. I saw her Crocs lying on the bathroom floor, where she'd just kicked them off after her soccer game earlier that evening, and I noticed they had Sharpie marker all over them. I was irritated that she'd decided to scribble all over her brand-new Crocs, so I picked them up to see what kind of nonsense she thought was important enough to vandalize her own shoes. And that's when I saw that she had written Bible verses all over those Crocs, verses about being strong and brave and trusting God with all your heart, mind, and soul. I nearly sat down on the bathroom floor and wept. She was in the midst of what had been one of the hardest seasons she'd been through in her fifteen years. She was dealing with mean girls and sports injuries and grade stress and social pressure—all the things we want to protect our kids from and pray they won't face. Yet what I realized in that moment was that she had actually been listening to Perry and me as we encouraged her to find her strength in God and to lean on him. She found verses that spoke to her and wrote them on her shoes in permanent marker as a reminder. Sometimes the very best part of parenting is when you let go and watch what your child has learned.

You know what else I've realized? More than anything else, kids want our time. They want to know that we hear them and that we value them. Yes, between the ages of thirteen and twenty, they may act annoyed when we get in their business, but deep down they really want to know we are paying attention. Teenagers are way too cool to yell, "Hey, Mom! Watch me jump off the diving board!" but they have a version of it that comes in an unspoken form, and you have to be paying attention to notice it. In our house, that often happens after 11:00 at night when I can barely function and Caroline is suddenly a hungry philosopher in need of therapy, but I've learned I can't choose when she decides to tell me what's really going on and gives me a window to her heart, so I take it where I can get it. I'll sleep when I'm fifty. Maybe. Except for the hormones. And the fact that I'll still worry about my child when she doesn't live under my roof.

Sometimes I can get distracted from what is happening in the moment by thinking more about who Caroline will become. Will she be happy? Will she be kind? Will she contribute to the world in fulfilling ways? Will she take risks? Will she ever learn how to put her dirty clothes in the hamper? That's when I remind myself that the best way to guarantee those traits is to focus not on who she will become, but on who she is right now.

We have eighteen years to listen and teach and admonish and praise. Waking up every day to love our babies, to learn from them, to fall and get back up again, to do life together in all its messy glory is a gift that shapes each of us forever, no matter what the future brings.

We need to stay emotionally connected to our kids in every stage of the parenting journey. When we are present in their lives, we know who they are. We know their weaknesses, strengths, struggles, and triumphs. And they'll trust us to have their best interests at heart because they'll see how much we care about them. They'll know they are valued, and they'll know they can use us as "the bad guy" to give themselves an out when they need it. They may not admit it at the time, but part of them knows we aren't trying to ruin their social lives as much as guide them to make good choices and help them figure out a better way when they don't. They may not want to hear our one-millionth lecture about Snapchat and how we live in a world where they need to assume everything they say and do is being recorded, but we can hope they'll take us seriously because nobody sets out to be the latest viral scourge of the earth.

They need to see we're their biggest fans and that we love them for who they are and who they are becoming. It's in the quality time that we keep the doors of communication open and get them to talk to us and, most importantly, trust us. Sometimes we need to put down our computers and our phones and forget about the to-do list and just listen.

Most of all, we need to pray for wisdom and discernment as we raise these kids because, ultimately, God knows them and loves them more than we do. In James 1:5, we are told to ask God for wisdom, so let's ask. Pray for your kids. Fight a culture that wants to tell them at every turn how they need to conform, and teach them how to be a bright light in a dark world.

* * *

Gulley used to teach at a Christian preschool, and one day, after she'd shared the story of Jesus's crucifixion and resurrection with the class, one of her three-year-old students told her mom that at school they'd heard, "A sad story and a happy story and a mad story" as she relayed the story of Jesus's betrayal by friends, the crucifixion, and the joy of Mary Magdalene finding the empty tomb. This is also a good description for being the mom of a teenager because it's an almost constant combination of feeling sad one minute, happy the next, and mad a minute later when you realize they lied when they said their room was clean.

It also looks a lot like being a combo Uber driver/ATM machine who dispenses cash at will. Stay tuned for my TED Talk on raising a teenager entitled, "I don't know what time it starts or where I'm going or who's going to be there and I'm annoyed you're so concerned over minor details and please quit saying 'That's lit.'" There's really no experience like having the child to whom you have dedicated your whole heart and soul text you, "GTG" (got to go), when you care enough to text them and ask how their day is going at school. They also give up after three seconds of looking for the tennis shoes that you know are in their closet but will devote forty-five minutes to answering questions for an online hair quiz to determine their hair texture and which expensive products they think you should buy them to help them live their best hair life.

Here's a teen math problem for you that perfectly illustrates this stage of life. If you have six half-full water bottles in your bedroom, how long will it take to walk to the fridge and get a seventh one? If you left four pairs of shoes in the kitchen and then grab another pair out of your closet, how many pairs of shoes will you eventually leave in the kitchen? Also, one pair of soccer cleats left in your backpack long enough equals a great science fair exhibit on the danger of staph infections.

I was in Starbucks a while back, and another mom was there with her toddler. The whole time they were in line, the little girl kept up a running commentary on everything, and clearly wanted her mom's full attention. "Mommy, look at me! Mommy, see how I picked out my own juice? Mommy! Mommy! Mommy!"

Those days are a vague memory now that parenting often feels more like being a groupie at a Justin Timberlake concert and you're just hoping maybe you'll get ten seconds of eye contact.

A few days ago, Caroline and I went shopping for a homecoming dress. We went to Dillard's at the mall closest to our house, and I prayed that God, in his infinite mercy, would let us find a dress without too much pain and agony. *Lord, have mercy on me, a mother in the juniors' party dress section of a department store that has seen better days.* Caroline and I went our separate ways and each began pulling dresses that we thought might work. It's safe to say our choices looked significantly different. Mine was compiled of offerings that looked as though they came from the Barbie Princess collection and hers was more like The Kardashians Do Homecoming. How else do you describe a crushed velvet dress in a size zero that looks like it's not big enough to be used as a dust rag?

We eventually made our way to the dressing room, where I asked if I should come in or if she wanted me to sit outside. She invited me in, and so I silently followed with all the awe and privilege that being allowed into a teen girl's private sanctum requires. I'd gone to see the musical *Hamilton* a couple of weeks earlier, and all I could think was, *I am in the room where it happens.*

Caroline began to try on dress after dress. I dutifully zipped up each one, watched her make a face as she assessed it in the mirror, and then hung the reject back on the hanger, creating a large pile of no-thank-yous. All around us in the other dressing rooms, I could hear moms and daughters engaging in the same discussions we were.

Mom: I *love* that one! It's just precious!
Teen Girl: *Mother*, I do not want *precious*. I look like
    an American Girl doll. It's awful.
Mom: That one is perfect!
Teen Girl: It is not perfect! It feels like *daggers on my*
    skin! Help me get it off! It's like *daggers*.

It occurred to me that a brilliant business plan would be to find a way to sell wine in the juniors section of department stores across America during homecoming and prom season. When it comes to finding the right party dress, mothers across the nation have never known less about fashion or style or what looks best. Any pride we ever had in our ability to make sartorial selections is decimated faster than you can say, "Gunne Sax by Jessica McClintock."

About this time, Caroline tried on a black, ruffled dress that I'd brought in as a last-ditch Hail Mary. She wrinkled her nose when she saw it, but I told her it would look much better on than it did on the hanger and encouraged her to just try it. I zipped up the back for her, she looked at herself in the mirror for a long few minutes, and then turned to me and asked, "What do you think?"

What do I think?

I think you are my sun and my moon, and no light shines

brighter than you in my life. I think I blinked, and my little girl became a gorgeous woman who makes me so proud I can hardly bear it. I think you are the most amazing, perfect creature who has ever been made and I can't believe I've had the privilege of raising you. I think you are leaving for college in just a few short years, and I have no idea how I can't remember life before you, yet have never seen time go by so fast. I think that I hope I've prepared you for life and for the challenges you'll face as you find your way. I think you are every dream I ever had standing in front of me in a black, ruffled dress.

But I couldn't say all that. She would just roll her eyes and never understand until one day when, God-willing, she has a daughter of her own.

So I just said, "Babe, you look stunning! It looks great on you. That's the perfect dress!"

She replied with a shrug of her shoulders, and said, "Eh, I don't know. I think I'll go with the other one instead."

And that sums up having a teenager. These are the years that increase our prayer life as we hold on for the ride to see who they are going to become and try to figure out how to show them the way and get out of their way all at the same time.

Mamas, remember this. We are cracked. We are flawed. We are far from perfect. We won't always get it right, and there will be plenty of days when we just put our heads down and cry at all the ways we messed up. We will give lectures that just ramble on about character and perseverance and doing unto others as you would have done unto you and hope we've made some kind of point. Yet God entrusted these babies to us because of that and, honestly, in spite of that. We are the ones he knew could shape them into the people he created them to be.

On the bright side, I choose to believe it's keeping my mind sharp by forcing me to find ways to keep my sanity while my child has the audacity to honk the car horn at me to hurry up like my only job in life is to be her chauffeur.

CHAPTER 7

THE BRIGHT SIDE OF
MAKING GOOD
FASHION CHOICES

*Don't be into trends. Don't make
fashion own you, but you decide what
you are, what you want to express by
the way you dress and the way to live.*

—GIANNI VERSACE

I picked up Caroline from school yesterday, and as we were waiting for the light to turn green, we couldn't help but notice a high school girl walk past us wearing running shorts and a T-shirt. Her backpack had caused her shorts to hike all the way up, along with her shirt, and so you could actually see her bare bottom. Like both cheeks. And she was just walking along about to head down a major street. I turned quickly at the light, put my car in park, and jogged to catch up with her, not entirely sure what a person is supposed to say in such a situation. I went with, "Hey, sweetie, your backpack has caused your shorts to ride up in the back and you can see your bottom." She looked at me for just a brief second and then said, "Okay," as she kept on walking and did nothing to address her shorts situation. I cannot stress enough that you could see her bare bottom. This wasn't a case of booty shorts, it was a case of booty.

Is this what fashion has become? I mean, I'm aware that all the young girls are currently wearing oversized T-shirts with shorts that make it appear as if all they have on is a T-shirt, and I get that. I lived that same trend myself back in the mid-eighties and still have the oversized Frankie Say Relax T-shirt to prove it. But I don't believe full-on cheeks are ever acceptable. Nobody wants to see your bare bottom. I don't even want to see my own bare bottom. I've managed to spend the bulk of my life not looking at my bottom in the mirror. I realize that J-Lo and the Kardashians (single-bottomedly?) made curvy rear ends a thing, and that's all well and good, but that doesn't mean we need to start letting them hang out of our drawers.

For a woman who is now facing the dark side of her forties, these are confusing fashion times. Target is currently selling acid-washed jeans and those brightly colored wind suits we all wore in the early 1990s and which made us look like very sporty senior citizens. High-waisted jeans are back, and crop tops are in. As God is my witness, ten years ago I vowed I'd never wear a belt again, and now they've made a comeback. I was ready to wear tunics with leggings forever, yet the arbiters of the fashion world had to go screw it all up and not let me live my one life. I'm too old to go back to the neon of my youth, yet too young to completely let it go and get myself a polyester housecoat like my Me-Ma used to wear.

I began following all of these fashion bloggers on Instagram to help me figure out what to wear and how I should wear it in the hopes of staying current, but here's what I've discovered. They are all the approximate size of a Calico Critter. This was a shocking discovery because most of them appear to be a somewhat normal size in their photos. Or maybe I just have extreme body joy and think we are the same size. I don't want to examine that too closely. I'll see them in their cute OOTD (that's "outfit of the day," as the kids say these days) and decide that I, too, can wear a cropped chambray jumpsuit with ruffles, only to discover I look more like Justin Timberlake circa 2001 when he and Britney Spears showed up at the American Music Awards in matching denim suits. It wasn't a good look for him then, and it's not a good look for me now. But I'll keep following along to check out a blogger's "Amazon haul" or "American Eagle try-on sesh" until I finally hear her say, "Guys, I had to order these jeans in a size 24."

I didn't wear a size 24 in elementary school.

Polly Pocket has to wear a size 25. That's a true story.

All of a sudden, it makes sense why she looked darling in those jeggings with her shirt tucked in and a belt while I looked like a sausage with a black strap around its middle to hold in its casing. We are not working with the same situation.

I do a regular feature on my blog called Fashion Friday. I've done it weekly for so long that some of these fashion bloggers were probably still wearing onesies from Gymboree when I started. And it's always just been links and stock photos of cute things I saw either in the store or online. It had never even occurred to me to take pictures of myself in the items until a few months ago, when a retailer contacted me to ask if I'd be interested in shopping at their store and then posting pictures of myself in their clothes.

This was so far out of my comfort zone that I couldn't even see my comfort zone. I didn't know how to pose. I didn't know where to look at the camera. I don't know how to take selfies. I can't figure out how people manage to film try-on stories and talk at the same time when I can't even hold my phone and push the right button to start recording.

I finally resorted to having Caroline take pictures of me in the outfits I'd picked out, and let's just say it wasn't the most glamorous of photo shoots. My photographer was impatient with my outfit changes and kept telling me she had chemistry homework. As if that's more important than taking pictures of your mom for the internet.

Anyway, by the time it was over, I was exhausted. I have a whole new respect for fashion bloggers who do this day after day. It's a lot of effort to get dressed and figure out how to pose.

I mean, I didn't even do it right or have a Starbucks cup to hold and it was exhausting. I guess I'll never figure out how to get the perfect shot that includes my steering wheel, my trendy Nike sneakers, my perfectly manicured nails painted with "Funny Bunny," and a bouquet of peonies across my lap. You can teach an old dog how to microblade her face, but you can't teach her all your Instagram photo tricks.

* * *

I'm not sure at what point in my life I became aware of designer labels, but since I am a child of the seventies, there were some crucial, foundation-building years of my life that came about during the advent of Gloria Vanderbilt putting her family name on every bottom in America. I'm just saying, it could've influenced me.

I remember the day I graduated from wearing Garanimals to Luv-Its. Oh, you know you remember Luv-Its. My favorite pair had an ice cream cone stitched on the back pocket, and let's just say I was feeling myself at The Magic Skate in my sweet, sweet Luv-It jeans and my white skates with green pom-poms. Look out, world, because here I come, and I've got dessert embroidered on my bottom.

When my Luv-Its and their embroidered pockets became a little too childish, it was time to make way for Gloria Vanderbilt and that iconic swan. I had to have a pair. My Me-Ma took me shopping at the White House (a department store in Beaumont, Texas, not the house where the president lives) and bought me a pair of aqua (I would say turquoise, but we all know it was the seventies, and aqua is more appropriate) Gloria Vanderbilt jeans with a matching aqua Gloria Vanderbilt top, complete with elastic waistband. If ever there is a person in your life who will take you to buy an overpriced outfit, it's your grandmother who adores you. And if ever an outfit was designed to take fifth grade by storm, that was it. I wore those aqua jeans with—wait for it—my Yo-Yo sandals and a calico print rabbit fur coat for school pictures that year. I was basically a ten-year-old version of Snoop Dogg minus a cane.

Then tragedy struck. There are some moments a girl never forgets, and I can still picture the whole scene. I was sitting on the shag carpet in our living room, wearing my prized Gloria Vanderbilt ensemble and changing the batteries in my eight-track tape player (Is that the most 1970s sentence ever written?), when I looked down and realized I had gotten battery acid on my aqua jeans. They were ruined. To say I was upset is an understatement. What ensued was a display of prepubescent hormones that could serve as a warning label to anyone who will ever come in contact with a ten-year-old girl. And it clearly scarred me, because I have a phobia about changing batteries on various devices to this day.

Fortunately, Jordache jeans came in style shortly thereafter, and my heartache was assuaged by that little horse head on the front pocket of my jeans. Throughout my teenage years, I pined for Polo shirts, complete outfits by Esprit, Guess overalls, Laura Ashley dresses that made me look like a sailor, and Dooney & Bourke purses. No trend was left unturned.

One Christmas when I was in college, my boyfriend bought me a real Fendi purse. I don't even want to think about what he paid for it. I adored that purse. I carried it everywhere, and it lasted much longer than the relationship with the guy who bought it for me in the first place. Even after we broke up, I couldn't bring myself to get rid of the Fendi. It just looked too good with everything I owned, and it would be wrong to ditch a nice handbag because of a bad boyfriend.

Please see my website for information about booking me to give inspirational speeches to women.

I carried that Fendi bucket bag for about a year and a half before the leather on the drawstring began to erode. I couldn't believe such a nice purse was falling apart after a measly year and a half. So one day, when I was shopping at The Galleria in Houston, I noticed the Fendi store and marched right in there with my purse, confident that it gave me instant credibility.

I explained that my purse was about a year and a half old and the leather was falling apart. The saleswoman took my purse, gave it (and me) a withering once-over, and then said, in a snooty, faux French accent, "Well, this is obviously just a department store Fendi." It was like I had handed her a dead possum in Fendi clothing. She followed up with a condemning, "Our Fendis are not meant for everyday use, so there is nothing that can be done."

Of course. Because who wants to use a nice designer purse every day? That's madness.

✳ ✳ ✳

One of the greatest things that has happened to fashion over the last ten years is the athleisure trend. It's hard to believe now that there was a day when people didn't walk around in workout clothes all day long, whether or not they'd actually worked out. "Did I work out today? Yeah, I did. I worked out those cookies in my pantry."

Specifically, I have been blessed by the return of sweatpants.

Oh sure, they are calling them "joggers" now, to placate those of us who have experienced sweatpants before. But make no mistake—these are straight up, elastic-at-the-ankles sweatpants. Sweats. Stretchy pants in the vein of Nacho Libre, who informed us that, "When you are a man, sometimes you wear stretchy pants in your room. It's for fun."

The first pair of sweatpants I ever loved were from my junior high days. They were royal blue, with "Bammel Patriots" written on them in red. I wore them constantly, even after we moved to Beaumont and I no longer attended Bammel Middle School. Eventually, I moved on to other pairs. I remember a blue pair with a bear on them that I wore to school far more often than was probably socially acceptable, and then a pair of gray sweats that were part of the workout uniform for the high school dance team and which came with a matching hoodie. My daughter now wears this same outfit to school on cool days, except her sweats are for the soccer team and not the dance team. And then, during my freshman year at Texas A&M, I treated myself to a pair of maroon sweats with "AGGIES" written down the leg, and really believed I was living my best life. But at some point during my college tenure, cotton sweatpants fell out of favor and were traded in for the more elegant and sophisticated "wind suit."

I don't recall that the wind suit phenomenon lasted for very long, which is shocking because (insert sarcastic tone here) we all looked so good in them. But I do remember transitioning to some sort of wide-legged drawstring waist gray cotton pants in the late nineties, before J-Lo and Juicy Couture brought us the wonder that was the velour tracksuit in the early 2000s.

Don't be fooled by the velour tracksuit; I'm still Jenny from the block. Or a middle-aged woman who probably shouldn't have had "JUICY" written across my rear end in any scenario. But there were soon a million versions of the velour tracksuit, and I embraced the tracksuit trend because it was like pajamas you could wear to the grocery store. And then the velour began to go away, and we were left with the standard black yoga pant. Practical, comfortable, and generally acceptable in polite society. I wore yoga pants with wild abandon.

However, at some point in the last couple of years, the yoga pant seemed to transition into workout leggings/tights. This is all good and fine, except workout leggings and tights aren't as comfortable or forgiving as yoga pants and all of their afore-mentioned predecessors. Don't get me wrong; they're great for working out and are even perfect for Saturday morning soccer games or trips to the grocery store. But they are a little restrictive when you just want a comfy option in which to watch college football and eat chips and queso.

In fact, Gulley and I had this exact discussion about a year ago. I'd gone over to her house to watch the Aggie football game wearing a pair of loose-fitting flare jeans with flip-flops and an Aggie T-shirt. She liked my jeans, but I told her I really wanted a more comfortable option, yet the jeans were the best I could do. We both agreed that what we really needed was a sweatpants option—something that offered the comfort of an elastic waist-band but without the judgment that comes when you wear actual pajama pants in public.

Why did we ever decide we were too good for some fleecy cotton with elastic at the ankles? As we continued our discus-sion, I told Gulley I didn't want us to get our hopes up, but I had seen signs that sweatpants were making a legitimate comeback. However, we would need to call them joggers because, in the words of Jerry Seinfeld, "You know the message you're sending out to the world with sweatpants? You're telling the world, 'I give up. I can't compete in normal society.'"

I'll tell you what sweatpants need. They need to hire the same PR person kale and cauliflower hired a few years ago.

As I continued to think about sweatpants, I realized we've actually been on the path to return to my first loungewear love for a while. Often in life, you find that the road you are on is the very road that will lead you back home. I believe sweatpants are like a hug for your legs, and I think we could all use a good hug right now in light of the fact that we are living in a time when it seems as if the whole world has lost its mind along with its collective good sense and reason. Plus, sweatpants, aka joggers, pair nicely with Netflix and a glass of wine. What more could you ask for in an article of clothing?

Nothing, that's what.

* * *

One morning when Caroline was about four, I got her dressed for school. She was wearing a hot pink outfit off of which she had eaten some bedazzles the last time she'd worn it, so it was clearly a favorite in many ways. I told her I was going to fix her hair in a new style, and I put part of it up with a bow and left the rest down. She ran into the bathroom to check out her new look, examined herself from every angle in the mirror, and finally said with a deep sigh, "Oh man, people are going to tell me *all day long* how beautiful I look." As if the very thought of all those compliments was just wearing her out.

That is my wish for all of us, that kind of confidence—says

the woman who is currently sitting on the couch in her Gap pajama bottoms and a T-shirt that reads, "The Best Life." I'm a study in irony.

I will leave you with five basic items of clothing I think everyone needs:

1. *A good white T-shirt.* This is a basic building block for a wardrobe. You can find a good white T-shirt for less than $10 on Amazon. It's the perfect layer under a sweater or jacket, or by itself. You can wear it with jeans or with the beloved joggers.

2. *A great pair of jeans.* Listen. You have to kiss a lot of frogs to find your prince. Go to a good department store, such as Nordstrom, and ask the sales clerk to help you find the right jeans for your body type. We are living in an age of denim freedom where you can choose from flare leg, skinny leg, high-rise, or moderate rise. You can wear dark denim, faded denim, or colored denim. The possibilities are endless. And I will tell you that my best jeans are the ones I spend more money on, and they are absolutely worth the investment. Don't judge me for how much I spend on jeans. I can spend whatever I want. You're not my real mom, Judy.

3. *A comfortable, stylish pair of shoes.* These can be whatever fits your lifestyle. There are sneakers with wedge heels now. You can wear boots, boot shoes, slip-on sneakers, or sandals. Even mules are making a comeback. Go with God and Dr. Scholl in your shoe options, and find something that works for you. Just make sure you can wear them all day without wanting to cut off your feet.

4. *A sweater coat, lightweight jacket, denim jacket, or trench coat.* Here's the thing about most women—if the temps plummet to somewhere around 70 degrees, then we are going to need a "light jacket." So make sure you have a cute one in your closet. It can be sporty, or it can be a sweater coat. There are no rules here. You can walk in light jacket freedom and find an option you love and can throw on everywhere from the ballpark to the movie theater.

5. *A black dress.* At some point in your life, no matter how casual, you will need a black dress. Or, at the very minimum, a nice pair of black pants. These are the kinds of things you can never find in stores when you actually need them, so you should always have some variation of these items waiting in your closet. When you find an attractive option for either of these wandering around in the wild, you should go ahead and purchase it immediately. You will thank me later.

The older I get, the more I realize it doesn't really matter what you wear or if it's the latest and greatest style. What I'd like is for each one of us to feel self-confident and comfortable in our own skin when we walk out the door every day in the clothes that work for us. Maybe even feeling so good that we dread all the compliments we'll get that day.

That's the bright side. Well, that and joggers.

CHAPTER 8

THE BRIGHT SIDE OF
HOLDING OUR
PLANS LOOSELY

*Some of us think holding on makes us
strong, but sometimes it is letting go.*

—HERMAN HESSE

It was the great philosopher Kenny Rogers who imparted this wisdom to us in his song, "The Gambler," back in 1979: "You've got to know when to hold 'em, know when to fold 'em. Know when to walk away and know when to run." He also told us we should never count our money while we're sitting at the table and regaled us with a cautionary tale about women named Lucille who might leave you with four hungry children and some crops in the field, but those are lessons for another day. Today is about knowing when it's time to move on to a new season.

You know what one of my biggest struggles is? Letting go of things. It's hard for me to surrender the things I love or want and trust that God wouldn't ask me to unless he had something bigger and better planned. Author and pastor Tim Keller says, "We can be sure our prayers are answered precisely the way we would want them to be answered if we knew everything God knows." And I totally agree with that, but it is still hard to trust when you can't see the whole story from beginning to end. No matter how much we want things to stay the same, life is always going to bring change. There are times when it's for the better, but honestly, sometimes it's not.

A couple of years ago, I was in the middle of writing my book, *Church of the Small Things*, when Perry and I began to feel God was calling us to literally start a small worship gathering in our community. We had attended the same church for almost twenty years, loved it and felt at home there, but we also knew

God was leading us to create something new in our neighborhood. This is the thing about God: every time I write a book on a certain topic, I discover it's that exact part of my life I'll get tested on. It's like God's making me put my words into actual actions. That's why my next book will be called, *The Struggle of Living on the Italian Riviera for a Year with a Budget of One Million Dollars.* Test me on that, Lord. I'm ready.

So, along with another couple who felt a similar calling, we started a Sunday morning worship service we called Community Worship. I know. The name is so catchy and original. We really stretched to come up with it. And for the next almost-three years, we met every Sunday in a small art studio that we'd been fortunate enough to rent for a reasonable price. During that time, countless people walked through our doors. Some stayed for the whole three years, some came for a few Sunday mornings, and some spent a few months or a year with us and then moved on. But what we began to notice about everyone who walked through our doors was that they had all been hurt in some way by the traditional church. For some, it was as simple as being burned out, but for others it was as complicated as feeling like they had never belonged or could find their place. Community Worship felt non-threatening. We had no real rules or guidelines. We didn't have a long-term plan. There were no ushers wearing brass-plated name tags to greet you at the door. We did have coffee because we aren't savages, but most of the traditional church trappings were nowhere to be found. We were just broken people who loved Jesus and wanted to help other broken people experience his love and grace and mercy. The end. We didn't have a mission statement, but if we did, that would have been it. Our worship was led by the other couple, who simply played a guitar and sang. Perry taught the bulk of Sunday mornings, and his messages were practical, straight from the Bible, and full of hope and grace. We did offer both gluten-free and full-gluten Jesus for Communion, so I guess we had that going for us as well.

If you ask Perry and me about those three years, you'll get different answers. He loved every minute of it. He loved teaching, he loved leading, he loved the preparation each week and was happy to get there early to set up chairs and make coffee and greet people and make small talk. For me, it was more of a struggle. I loved it and I loved being a part of it, but it also drained me. Before our time at Community Worship, I'd never even considered how people get the grape juice into those tiny plastic cups, and now I know there's a special dispenser you can order from Amazon that gets the job done.

Maybe it was because I had a lot of other ministry commitments at the same time, or maybe it's because I tend to be more of an introvert, or probably it was some combination of those things. All I know is, I wouldn't be honest if I told you I loved every minute of it. I loved the idea of it. I loved knowing that we were being obedient and doing what God had called us to do. I loved the people who crossed our path during that time. I loved watching Perry use his gifts. Yet I continually questioned how long we could keep it going and wondered what God's endgame with the whole thing was.

I will tell you this: God used that time to stretch me and challenge me and make me take a hard look at myself and the ways I can be selfish and focused on my own comfort. I can talk a good game about taking up my cross and dying to self, but the truth is, I also like to stay in bed late some Sunday mornings, and I don't always know the best way to reach out to people and make them feel loved. These are things I had to admit to myself, and it hurt my own feelings. It gave me a new appreciation for pastors and church volunteers and the people who make it all happen Sunday after Sunday. Church can be beautiful and healing, but it can also be messy and complicated because we are humans doing our best imitation of what we think God wants us to do—and we don't always get it right.

✳ ✳ ✳

We live in the same community where Perry grew up. It's funny how that happened, considering he never really planned on returning to the place where he was born and raised, but it is a borderline epidemic in our neighborhood, which is a testament to what a great place it is to live and raise a family. The fact that you choose to go back to a place where people knew you when you were awkward and had braces on your teeth, and remember the time you backed over the neighbor's mailbox with your car, can be humbling. It's also why we are living in his hometown and not mine.

Anyway, because Perry grew up here, it's pretty common for us to run into people he went to high school with, and Perry will be the first to tell you that he's come a long way since then. I think most of us had a hard time being our best selves in high school (please see above sentence about awkward and braces and backing over a neighbor's mailbox). For the most part, the friends we've made as adults in our community are people we met later in life, either in college or as we raised our babies together.

But I'm going to tell you a story that begins twenty years ago, when Perry and I were newlyweds. I left town with Gulley on New Year's Eve in 1998 because we were both going to be attendants in our friend Meredith's wedding on January 2, 1999. The wedding was in Kilgore, Texas, and the guest list consisted largely of people we both knew from college, so Gulley and I decided it would be more fun to just go together and leave our new husbands at home. I also think this had something to do with the wedding date falling right in the middle of hunting season. All that to say, I don't remember either of them begging us to let them attend the wedding.

We made the seven-hour drive to Kilgore and headed straight to the rehearsal dinner, which meant we didn't check into our hotel until later that night. And when I called home to check on Perry, he didn't have good news for me. Here's how I knew this. He started the conversation with, "Well, I'm lying in bed, and my mom had to come take care of me." This is really what a new wife wants to hear to feel spectacularly good about her wife skills.

As it turned out, Perry had been in our backhouse—basically a garage but with a small room attached that serves as his man cave—cleaning up guns and straightening up tools and such. Truth be told, I don't know what he was doing, but these are the things I imagine he does in the backhouse based on the three times I've walked out there during our marriage. Anyway, he bent down to pick up a piece of paper that fell on the ground and his back went out. As in, he was lying on the ground and couldn't move. He couldn't reach his cell phone to call anyone, so he lay there and tried to figure out how he was going to make it into the house or find anyone to help him get up.

Then he looked up and saw a childhood friend of his jogging by and, in desperation, he yelled out, "Trey! Hey, Trey! Over here! It's Perry Shankle." Fortunately, Trey wasn't freaked out by the sound of a voice that appeared to be coming from nowhere and ventured into our backyard to see what was going on. He found Perry lying there on the backhouse floor and helped him get up and into the house, then waited until Perry's mom got there to take care of him. Perry counts this as one of his life's lowest moments, and he'll be so thrilled I chose to share it here.

Perry recovered—he just needed some muscle relaxers and a day in bed. I got home a couple of days later, and he told me what happened and how his friend Trey had helped him. And even though he lived just a few blocks away, we didn't see Trey again for another twenty years after that. We heard through the grapevine that he'd gotten divorced, and then we heard he'd gotten remarried. We'd see him and his new wife, Kim, across the room at the occasional social gathering, and that was about the extent of it.

I'm sure you're wondering where this story is going and how it relates to Community Worship, so let's make that circle. We had been doing Community Worship for about a year when, one Sunday, Trey walked in with Kim and their combined kids. Trey has two boys and a girl from his first marriage, and Kim has two daughters from hers. We all visited after the service was over that morning, and although I wasn't sure they would ever come back, they ended up being with us almost every single Sunday at Community Worship for the next two years.

Perry and Trey had grown up together. They were so close as kids that Perry spent the night at Trey's house the night after Perry's dad passed away. They had all this shared history but had drifted away from each other over the course of life. Now they were back in each other's lives on a weekly basis. Kim has become a dear friend to me, like an honorary big sister. Her girls are just a little bit older than Caroline, and she has been invaluable in encouraging me as I try to figure out all that parenting a teenage girl entails. Her girls surrounded Caroline and loved her through one of the hardest years of her life. They came into our life because they walked through the doors of Community Worship. If not for that, I don't know that any of us would ever have connected, but we are all better for it.

Here's what I learned: it's in the pouring out of yourself that you most often find yourself filled up in ways you could never anticipate or expect. The majority of people who passed through Community Worship were people we would never have known otherwise. Perry and I look back at the time and see how it really served as something best described as a "Church ICU" where people came who had been hurt by the church or whose faith had been shaken by hard things in life and that little art studio became a place where God made them whole again and equipped them to move on to the next chapter of their lives. They needed a safe place to land after surviving some fierce storms. God used what we were doing to help them, but he also used them to change us and make us better than we'd been before. So many families offered support, love, and encouragement. There were a couple of kids who spent a whole summer afternoon doing a lemonade stand to raise money for our Sunday school class. There were a few older couples who came in early to help us set up chairs or brought donuts or asked how they could pray for us. Just countless things that may have not seemed like much but helped encourage us more than they will ever know. Ultimately, there is nothing in life that matters more than community, being loved and loving others in return.

* ** *

It was just shy of the three-year mark for Community Worship when Perry and I began to feel like maybe it had run its course. We couldn't figure out why, exactly, but it was definitely a sense we both had, so we began to pray about it. The odd thing was that I had finally embraced Community Worship in both my heart and mind over that last year, so it seemed weird to think about walking away from it. We agreed that we would wait and see what happened. Ultimately, several unmistakable events converged over the next week and made it clear it was time to move on. The chapter was over. I felt some combination of relieved, confused, and sad. It's still something I can't quite define. It was a season of ministry where we both knew we had done what we'd been called to do and seen God do some amazing things, but it's also a little jarring when one chapter ends and you aren't sure how the next begins. All we know is that it was time to let go and trust God with the rest.

Around that time, I was reading through Genesis, and I got to the story about Moses's mother, Jochebed, placing him in a basket in the Nile River in an attempt to save him from Pharaoh's order that all Hebrew baby boys under age three were to be killed. Jochebed somehow knew Moses wasn't an ordinary child; maybe she heard a whisper from God, letting her know he had great things in store for her baby boy. And so, by faith and in defiance of Pharaoh's order, she and her husband hid Moses for three months. Can you even imagine the stress of hiding a newborn for three months?

But the day finally came when Jochebed knew she could no longer hide him, so she had to do something even more difficult—she had to let her baby go and trust God with the rest. Jochebed put Moses in a basket, set him in the Nile, and let him go. She had to believe God had a purpose and a plan as she let her baby float away into the unknown. The thought of putting your helpless newborn in a basket in the Nile River kind of puts dropping your kids off at college in perspective. I mean, Moses didn't have white twinkly lights in that basket or anything.

Then, Pharaoh's daughter found Moses floating in his basket and decided to raise him as her son. Even better, she unknowingly chose his own mother, Jochebed, to nurse him. Moses ended up being raised in the most powerful household in all of Egypt, which paved the way for him to be the one God used to lead the Hebrew people out of slavery and captivity. The faithfulness of Jochebed in letting go of her baby, even when it didn't make sense and she didn't know how it would end, changed history.

We've all had to let go of things—dreams, relationships, opportunities. Sometimes it's easy to know when to walk away, but there are also times when it's gut-wrenching and filled with uncertainty. Life passes in seasons, and they change and end and begin again. The wisdom comes in knowing when to hold on and when to move on. Jochebed's story is a reminder that God is always working out better things for us than we can imagine. When we trust him and let go, even when we don't understand, he will give back to us far more than what we have given up for him.

These days we have returned to the church that had been our home for so many years before we began Community Worship, and I can see all the ways that it's the perfect fit for us in this season of our lives. As hard as it was to understand why Community Worship came to an end when it did, God has led us back to a place that feels like home, a place where we can grow and be challenged. He knew what we needed before we knew what we needed. He's good like that.

The bright side is holding our plans, hopes, and dreams with an open hand, remembering that often the things that are ahead are better than the things we left behind.

CHAPTER 9

THE BRIGHT SIDE OF
THINKING BEFORE SPEAKING

The secret of being boring is to say everything.

—VOLTAIRE

A few weeks ago, I had a typical Monday. You know, a lot of making lists and trying to get my week off to a productive start. Although I have to tell you that the only thing that gets me out of bed on Monday mornings is telling myself I'll go right back to bed after I get Caroline off to school. I never actually do this, but it's amazing how it soothes my psyche at 7:00 a.m. on a Monday.

As it happened, Perry took Caroline to school that day, Unbeknownst to me, he'd toasted himself an English muffin, covered it in peanut butter, and left it sitting on the counter-top. Meanwhile, I grabbed some dirty clothes out of our laundry baskets and put them in the washer, then loaded the dishwasher with all the breakfast dishes. When Perry walked back in the house about ten minutes later, he said, "You threw away my English muffin!"

I would never throw away someone's breakfast, so I replied, "I didn't even see your English muffin!" And that's when we both noticed Piper and Mabel lurking in the corner of the kitchen, looking guiltier than usual and profusely licking their lips. We can't prove it was them, but generally speaking, English muffins don't just disappear unless the rapture happened and said muffin believed in Jesus.

Anyway, instead of going back to bed, I drank a cup of coffee and worked on a few writing projects before I made a grocery list and a general to-do list. Then I went to work out at Smart Barre because I am currently trying to be the best version of myself. Afterward, I needed to run to the mail store to mail a few things, and since the mail store is right across the street from Target, I was overjoyed when I realized everything on my grocery list could be purchased at Target.

But once I found myself in Target, I ended up going down forty-seven rabbit trails, as one does when one finds oneself in Target. I looked at a few shirts, decided to go ahead and get snacks for Caroline's soccer game that weekend, and looked through the book section to see if anything looked interesting. Then Perry called and reminded me of a few more things we needed, and I spied the dollar aisle and went all, *Squirrel! Squirrel!*

All this to say, by the time I finally made my way to the checkout line, it was after 2:30 p.m., and I hadn't eaten lunch. I was starving. I decided I'd drive through Whataburger as soon as I left Target for a cheeseburger and a Diet Coke. I'd officially crossed into Chris Farley territory in the SNL skit where he says, "Lay off me, I'm starving!" as he eats french fries by the handful.

I found what appeared to be the shortest checkout line, except the guy in front of me couldn't get his microchip credit card to work in the reader. (I get that microchip cards are safe and secure and the wave of the future but—*serenity now*—because they never seem to work the same way twice.) Meanwhile, my stomach was basically eating itself. Then I realized that the cashier in the line I chose is one I have on a regular basis. And this is where I need to tell you that she is very sweet and very good at her job.

But here's the thing. Whenever I go to Target, I always buy these Dingo chew sticks for Piper and Mabel. And every time I have this cashier, she rings up those Dingo chew sticks and then says, "*Aw!* Do you have a dog at home? What kind?" I always smile and reply, "Yes, we have two dogs. They are Blue Lacys."

This leads to a litany of questions.

"What are Blue Lacys?"

"What do they look like?"

"What color are they?"

"Are they friendly?"

"Are they from the same litter?"

"Do they get along?"

"Who did they vote for?"

And so on, until she forgets that she's supposed to be ringing up my purchases while we visit.

So when I realized it was this cashier, I prepared myself for the questions as she scanned the chew sticks and determined that, in my current starved condition, I was not emotionally prepared for all the inevitable questions about Blue Lacys. Sure enough, she looked up at me and said, "*Aw!* Do you have dogs? What kind are they?"

Listen. I didn't even have to think twice about my plan of action. Which was to lie.

I looked right at her, thought about the most common breed of dog I know and replied, quickly and irrationally, "Labs." I lied about my dogs to the cashier at Target. Jesus is going to come back for a toasted English muffin covered in peanut butter and leave me behind.

And I don't need you to judge me. You were at my wedding, Denise.

In my defense, I was so hungry and just wanted to get to Whataburger and had truly crossed the line into hangry territory. I didn't want to talk about my dogs. I just wanted to pay for my groceries and pack of ten plastic coat hangers and seasonal candy and be on my way.

However, my nefarious ways did not pay off because she proceeded to ask, "What kind of labs?"

"How old are your labs?"

"How do you tell the difference between a lab and a golden retriever?"

"Are they from the same litter?"

"Have you seen that movie about a lab who plays basketball? Or was that a golden retriever?"

"What are their names?"

So what I'm telling you is, lying never pays off.

And I think Mabel sensed that I'd basically denied her at Target because when I got back home, she gave me the cold shoulder, and later I saw that she'd written a haiku:

> Lying is so wrong
> Worse than eating a muffin
> You make Jesus sad

That's right, Mabel. I'll never lie about having a lab again.

Also, my Whataburger was delicious, and I ate the whole thing in three bites.

* * *

Here's the thing about me—and I tell you this because you are my friend and I am comfortable with this personal character assassination of myself. I say a lot of dumb stuff. I'd like to pretend that my impulse to lie to a cashier at Target about what kind of dogs I own is a one-off kind of thing, but that's not really the truth. And it's not that I go around lying all the time as much as my mouth just gets ahead of my brain, and sometimes this leads to saying things I don't mean. I tend to talk at a speed that would be defined by *Schitt's Creek*'s Moira Rose as "rapid velocity." I'm often in need of a filter because my go-to is almost always to be funny, and sometimes funny and kind don't line up. Not to mention that I have a tendency to use a sarcastic remark to cut the emotional tension in a room, and that can come off as less than empathetic. It's not that I don't feel what someone else is feeling as much as I just want to figure out how to bring the mood up a notch.

A few years ago, Gulley and I went to the rodeo with a bunch of friends. We took several pictures while we were there, and the next day she asked, "Hey, will you text me that picture of the two of us?" And I replied, "I deleted that picture. It wasn't good of me and, I'll be honest, it wasn't any good of you, either." We now have a term we use when we're afraid one of us is about to be perfectly and honestly blunt: "Whisper it first." This comes from a friend of Gulley's whose mother used to beg her daughter to "Whisper it first" before she said something out loud because she was so prone to blurt out the verbal equivalent of a bull in a china shop.

When God told Moses to go to Pharaoh, Moses said, "Pardon your servant, Lord. I have never been eloquent, neither in the past nor since you have spoken to your servant. I am slow of speech and tongue." To which the Lord responded, "Who gave human beings their mouths? Who makes them deaf or mute? . . . Is it not I, the Lord? Now go; I will help you speak and will teach you what to say" (Exodus 4:10–12).

God himself promises to teach us what to say. We just have to listen and learn when to speak and when to keep our mouths shut. Because the thing is, the stuff we say comes from somewhere in our hearts, and the heart is the place of convictions, aspirations, dreams, values, hopes, cynicism, doubts, and all the emotions we bring to the table in any given situation.

Even as I write, I'm constantly thinking of the stories I can tell and the stories that aren't mine to tell. What's too personal? What could hurt someone I love? Author Anne Lamott once said, "If people wanted you to write warmly about them then they should have behaved better." While I love that quote in theory, it would play out in a not-so-healthy way in reality. So I edit myself constantly. I have also made the decision that there are a whole lot of stories I will eventually tell decades from now in a book called, *Now That Everybody's Dead*. If only I were as careful in everyday conversation as I am with the written word. But I guess the thing about the written word is that it's concrete proof of what I say. That's slightly terrifying because we now live in a world that will find something someone said ten years ago and obliterate them for it without even taking the time to consider if that's how they still feel or even what they originally meant.

We've all read horror stories about someone who Tweets something, probably impulsively, gets on a plane, and then lands hours later to discover they've been fired from their job and their whole life has blown up. There have never been more ways to put our words out there on display for people to see and judge what we meant to say or what they think we meant to say without giving us any benefit of the doubt. Our lives are built on words and, most importantly, our relationships are built on words and the grace we extend to each other. We seem to have forgotten that we can disagree and still love. Me calling you an idiot for your political beliefs isn't going to do one thing to change your mind; it will just change our relationship. We have to let the Spirit dwell in us so that we can have peace, patience, joy, love, kindness, and self-control. Imagine how different Twitter and the world would be if we all kept that in mind and acted even remotely reasonable and open to hearing someone else's point of view.

We can't take back our words. When someone says something mean, unkind, or untrue, it takes time to rebuild trust. Once it's out there, it's out there. From now on, the cashier at Target will always think I have labs. Unfortunately, that doesn't mean she will quit asking me a million questions about them every time I check out.

But thinking about all of this helps me to remember to pray:

> May these words of my mouth and this meditation of
> my heart
> be pleasing in your sight,
> LORD, my Rock and my Redeemer. (Psalm 19:14)

The bright side is knowing that our words are powerful and carry a heavy weight, which is why we need to do our best to use them wisely. Because, as the saying goes, "Better to remain silent and be thought a fool than to speak and to remove all doubt."

CHAPTER 10

THE BRIGHT SIDE OF
BEING BRAVE

*What would life be if we had no
courage to attempt anything?*

—VINCENT VAN GOGH

Perry and I often watch the evening news together. I can't tell you how sad I am to admit this publicly because has any sentence ever more clearly made me realize I am becoming my grandparents? At what point does that transition happen, and you begin to care about things such as the federal deficit and what's going on in the Middle East? When I was in fifth grade, my homeroom teacher gave us a weekly assignment to report on a current event. One week, I made an entire poster board dedicated to the assassination of Anwar Sadat, the president of Egypt, and my teacher was so impressed that I held on to the assassination of Anwar Sadat as my cornerstone of any conversation on world events for many years after. It was my fifth-grade version of a cocktail party topic. And, really, what group of elementary school students doesn't want to discuss the murder of a political leader around the swings at recess? Did I know or care what his assassination meant for the political world stage? Not even a little bit. But has my basic knowledge of this event served me well in a game of Trivial Pursuit? Yes, it has.

Anyway, I'm not sure how Perry and I landed on the nightly news as our evening programming, but the answer lies somewhere in the fact that we never want to watch the same thing on TV. He prefers anything on the Outdoor Channel, while my viewing habits veer toward anything that involves a group of single women vying for a rose or some housewives fighting on a luxury cruise ship.

And so, the news it is. But as the political climate has become increasingly volatile over the last couple of years—perhaps you've noticed—it seems all the news outlets are a lot more interested in ramping up our fear factor based on our political ideology and leanings versus actually telling us what's going on. I think it was at the end of last November when Perry and I noticed that the news anchors always cut to commercial break with some statement along the lines of, "Up next, find out what is happening right now that means America will NEVER BE THE SAME." That feels like a lot, right? I noticed that my anxiety level would steadily creep up as the night went on and, by the time I was ready to go to bed, I'd be so worried about North Korea or whatever that I couldn't sleep. And you know what I have no control over at midnight or ever? Kim Jong-un. There's not enough melatonin to combat that.

It's not just the news, though. We have become a culture that binges on fear-based click bait. All you have to do is look on any given internet site to see headlines about everything from super bacteria and kidnappings in plain sight to a kid who died from snorting a Tide Pod. And just when I think it's safe to peruse Facebook to see if a high school friend has posted her one hundredth picture from her vacation in the Bahamas, I stumble on an article about a kid who drowned eight hours after getting out of the pool. It's no wonder the pharmaceutical industry is selling anti-anxiety meds like they're corn dogs and lemonade at the state fair.

Everywhere we turn, we learn that our economy might bottom out, both political parties are trying to ruin us, our kids aren't safe walking down the street, and Alexa is listening to every conversation we have inside the walls of our homes and creating a document that might later be used against us in a court of law.

I was at Target the other day, buying my usual $100 of things I didn't know I needed, and when I went to check out, the cashier asked for my ID. I couldn't figure out why he needed my ID since I had, to my knowledge, not added wine to my cart. (Although, at Target, there is always the possibility that I unknowingly threw in a bottle of cabernet along with the Magnolia Home candle I couldn't resist and a set of Valentine's Day dish towels that were marked 50 percent off.) But somehow, I realized he needed my ID for the box of tampons I was buying. Tampons. I was so confused. So I went home and consulted Google, only to find out that kids are boiling tampons and drinking the "juice" that produces to get high.

First of all, *ew.*

Second of all, do better, kids of America.

But the point is, a thing I didn't even know existed just moments before had now become one more thing to my list of things to be worried about and to give parental safety lectures about. You know what you never imagine when you hold your precious infant in your arms? That one day you'll have to utter the phrase, "Don't get high off tampon juice."

About six months ago, I was in the middle of grocery shopping at my local H-E-B and got a call from my ob/gyn's office. This isn't a normal occurrence, and I'd just been there the week before for all my annual exams, so I decided I should answer right there in the frozen food section. The nurse on the other end of the line informed me that my mammogram revealed what appeared to be a small mass in my left breast. When could I come back in for further testing? And that's how I found myself having a panic attack right by the ice cream. I'd just lost my dear friend, Jen, to breast cancer six months earlier and was in the process of watching two other friends go through chemotherapy and radiation for small tumors that were found during their routine mammograms. I walked right out of H-E-B. Just left my cart right there full of groceries, got in my car, and put my head on the steering wheel. I've heard it said that you're usually not doing anything special when the pieces of your life fall apart, and that is exactly how I felt in that moment. I went straight to worst case scenario in an impressive 2.3 seconds.

As it turned out, a follow-up mammogram revealed that it was just a weird shadow. I have dense breasts that are apparently the mammogram version of looking through a Jell-O salad filled with chunks of pineapple, and now I have totally overshared. You didn't ask to know that about me. And I bet you'll never look at a Jell-O salad the same way again. I apologize.

Fear exists because we live in a broken world where so much is beyond our control. I read a joke once wherein God said to the angels, "Look! I've created man!" and the angels replied, "What you've done is mess up a perfectly good monkey. Look how anxious and fearful that thing is!"

But the hope within the story of our fear is the story of who is in control. And the truth is, it is not always wrong to feel afraid. We were definitely created to experience healthy fear, which keeps us from doing stupid things.

For example, when I was a sophomore in high school, I wasn't the most secure person in the world. If I could insert a photo here for you to see, it would explain a lot. I'll just sum it up by telling you that owning a fantastic pair of forest green Girbaud jeans can't make up for the tragic error of perming your bangs. I struggled with fitting in, trying to be much cooler than I was, and making good decisions. All the teenage girl basics.

My youth pastor's wife noticed I was having a hard time and invited me to go to Houston with her to go shopping for the day. This felt like a huge win because she was young, pretty, and basically everything I aspired to be at that time in my life. While we were on this shopping trip, I found myself in a store called Contempo Casuals. If you were a teen in the 1980s, then I'm going to give you a moment to recall the greatness of Contempo Casuals. It was essentially the precursor to Forever 21, and perhaps the original store that catered to teen girls who desperately wanted to channel their inner Madonna or Debbie Gibson. There, amongst all the plaid stirrup pants and oversized cut-up sweatshirts and jackets with shoulder pads that would make the cast of *Dynasty* feel alarmed, I found a zip-up denim dress.

Here's what you need to know about me: I have always been and will always be powerless to resist a denim dress. I have owned every variation of a denim—and its lesser cousin, chambray—dress. As I write this, hanging in my closet is a light denim shirt dress, which I wear on a regular basis. I can't explain my undying love of denim in dress form, but I feel the blame lies somehow at the feet of Ralph Lauren and his brand of Americana chic.

But getting back to 1987, that denim dress was the original denim dress of my heart. To this day, no other denim dress has compared to its fabulousness. It was long-sleeved, zipped all the way up the front, had shoulder pads, and hugged all my fifteen-year-old curves. In hindsight, it probably looked more like a denim wetsuit than a dress. However, I did not let the unforgiving nature of a long denim sleeve deter me from making it my own.

I wore it to school the following Monday, and as the kids these days would say, I was feeling myself. Nobody was going to tell me nothing. I had on my denim dress/wetsuit with a pair of red Nine West flats, and even my permed bangs seemed to respect the dress to the point of only curling up halfway on my forehead. And then tragedy struck. During lunch, a girl who was a constant frenemy throughout our high school years spilled red fruit punch all over the front of my dress. Was it an accident? I'm still not sure. But I reacted poorly. I ran to get paper towels from the lunch ladies and happened to pass by the table where my older boyfriend was sitting with all his senior friends. In a split second, I decided to stop at his table to tell him of my plight, and said the following words, which haunt me to this day: "That b&*% spilled fruit punch all over my f*&%ing dress!"

I know. It's a wonder I wasn't in juvie.

I blame the dress for both my potty mouth and ill-timed bravado. I can only surmise that the denim sleeves cut off circulation to my brain.

As soon as that profane statement left my mouth, I registered all the senior boys making sounds like, "Ooooh," and "Noooo," and naturally, I figured it was because I had them all mesmerized by my story and sheer cool factor. Until I felt a tap on my shoulder and realized our assistant principal, Mr. Bledsoe, was standing right behind me and had heard every word I'd just said. Can you say "detention"? I knew you could.

So I had to go home and break the news to my mother that not only did the shopping trip to Houston with the youth pastor's wife not have the intended effect on me, but it led to me buying a denim dress that caused me to say the F-word in front of a school administrator, resulting in a three-day detention.

This is what is known as healthy fear.

Side note: What a sweet, innocent time the 1980s were,

when a kid would get a three-day detention sentence for saying two bad words. I believe these days that's called "high school." You can say whatever you want; just don't get caught vaping while you say it.

I confessed my miscreant behavior to my mother in the drive-thru line at Burger King, which is where all the gravest sins have been confessed. Her response was, "I didn't know you even knew that word!" and then I was grounded for two weeks, during which time I intentionally found ways to get caught reading my Bible and underlining passages with colored pencils to prove how sorry I was, in hopes of getting time off for good behavior. That didn't happen, by the way.

Healthy fear is a good thing. Now that I'm raising a teenager of my own, I realize there needs to be some fear of consequences for bad behavior and decisions. It keeps us between the rails and, ideally, from spending time sitting in a depressing detention room. As adults, it can help us make good decisions and protect us from doing damage to our lives or the lives of others. It's like when you read about those kids who are born unable to feel physical pain and repeatedly injure themselves without realizing it. As humans, we need to be able to recognize fear and pain in order to give ourselves healthy boundaries.

But here's where it can become a problem: when we allow it to dwell in our hearts and homes, control our thought lives, our decisions, our relationships, and our parenting. What we do with our fear reveals what we really believe.

We find ourselves grasping for control and researching what could go wrong. We analyze statistics in an attempt to manage our fear or control what might cause it. I do this all the time when I read about tragedies. Was he wearing a helmet? Did they let their kid walk to school alone? Was she wearing sunscreen? I bet they drank too many Diet Cokes.

But what if, instead of the goal being to manage our fear, we decided to fight it? What if we just took a deep breath and said, "I'm not in control, but I trust the one who is"? I'm totally living in this place right now, by the way, as I am on the precipice of having a teen driver in my house. Do you need to exponentially increase your prayer life? Get yourself a teenager behind the wheel of a car. Caroline can't drive yet, but one of her friends just got her license last week, and I was paralyzed with fear when, a few days later, Caroline said, "Mom, Kate's going to come pick me up and we're going to go drive around and maybe go out to eat." I guess my face communicated my trepidation because she immediately followed that up with, "Don't worry! She made a ninety on her driving test!"

Oh. Well, why didn't you say that in the first place? I feel so much better now. Can we clarify what she lost ten points for, because I'm a lot more concerned about what she got wrong than what she got right.

The truth is that faith isn't the absence of fear—it's being afraid of doing that thing but doing it anyway. It's letting go of our kids, our finances, our marriage, and saying, "Here you go, God. I trust you with all of this." Instead, I have been guilty of spending a lot of time imagining worst case scenarios and going down roads that usually end up with us living in a van down by the river. Why is our human tendency to always envision impending doom? Or is that just me?

There will always be situations outside our control. And that's the point. God wants us in a place of trusting him to provide and to protect. It's no wonder we get so freaked out; we were never meant to handle it all alone. We need to remember these truths: God is good, God is ever present, God is sovereign, and God is full of grace and mercy and love for us.

This doesn't mean we'll never fight fear again, but it does mean we aren't fighting it alone. Here's the thing about God: he will always do what he says he will do, he promises that we are never alone, and he uses all things for good. He promised the children of Israel that they would be led into the Promised Land, but they continually doubted him. When God sent twelve men to go investigate the land he had for them, only two—Joshua and Caleb—came back believing they could take the land. The other ten saw only the obstacles and all the reasons it wouldn't work. They lost sight of God's faithfulness and let their fear take over. It was their land, but they had to be brave enough to take it. To take hold of the new, we have to face our fears and let go of the old.

When Caroline was in fourth grade, she walked into my bathroom late one night. She did it in that way little kids do, like a ninja about to attack, so I was startled when I looked up and saw her standing there. "What's wrong?" I asked, because as a mom, you learn early on that when a child appears suddenly late at night, there is always something wrong, whether it's real or manufactured.

She tearfully poured out, "I was in bed and I was reading your book, *Sparkly Green Earrings*, and you wrote about how sad you were when I went to kindergarten and how fast time goes by and now I'm sad because I don't want to ever leave you and Daddy and I only get to live at home for nine more years!" By the time she got to the end of that long statement, she was truly sobbing.

I wrapped her up in a hug and said, "Babe, that is so far away and not anything you need to worry about tonight. And I was sad when you started kindergarten, but I was excited, too. Remember how great it turned out to be and how much you loved Mrs. Cook and all the friends you made?" She nodded as she wiped her runny nose on my pajama top. "Life can seem scary when we think too far ahead or imagine what something will feel like. You aren't supposed to be ready to leave home when you're nine years old, but God is going to prepare you over the next nine years, and you'll grow and change and be ready for your future when it gets here. But tonight, all you have to do is close your eyes and go to sleep. You are safe and you are loved."

I tucked her back into bed, but as I walked back to my bedroom, God showed me how much I can be like that. I worry about the future. I worry about what others will think. I worry about the unknown and what might happen. I read the articles. I hear the news reports. We live in a world that feels scary, mainly because it is scary.

We can't always clearly see the path that lies before us, but that's the mystery of life. It's our opportunity to trust in a God who sees all things. The beginning. The end. The giants we will face. And everything in between.

Here's the bright side: we never have to face our fears alone.

CHAPTER 11

THE BRIGHT SIDE OF
LOVING OTHERS

*We show up for each other. That's what
we do.*

—GULLEY, MY BEST FRIEND

One night, when Caroline was about nine years old, Perry was in the backyard grilling steaks for dinner. We were just about to sit down to eat together. I pulled out the placemats and began to set the table. I put forks and sharp steak knives at the places where Perry and I always sit, but only a fork at Caroline's place. As we began to eat, Caroline asked, "Hey, where's my knife?" When I offered to cut her steak for her, Perry looked at me and said, "You realize I let her skin and butcher the deer she shot at the ranch last weekend, right?" Um, no, I did not realize that. That is terrifying.

In that moment, I realized the fundamental difference between what moms do and what dads do. I'm essentially trying to protect her from anything that could possibly cause her harm while Perry is turning her into our very own Bear Grylls. In the economy of parenting, dads tend to be the ones who encourage kids to take risks, accept challenges, and assert their independence. There's a poem by Erin Hanson with these lines:

> "What if I fall?"
> Oh but my darling,
> What if you fly?

Moms worry about the falling, and dads are the flight school instructors.

I adore my husband for the way he loves our girl. We found

out we were having a daughter when I was about twenty weeks pregnant, and from that moment on, there were always those people who asked if he'd hoped for a boy. Seriously? It's the 2000s. Are we still doing that?

Perry's answer was always the same: "I can do anything with a daughter that I could do with a son." And that's what he's done. I call them Big and Little Enos (I am never afraid of a *Smokey and the Bandit* reference) because she is his Mini-Me. He's taught her how to hunt, how to fish, how to throw a baseball and a punch. He's pushed her to take risks, try new things, and never accept that she can't do anything she sets her mind to do. They laugh at the same things, have the same smile, and share a kind of confidence in that if someone doesn't like them, it's clearly because something is wrong with that person. He has been Caroline's constant champion—there hasn't been a moment of her life when she's had to wonder if she is loved and adored by him. Perry is the very definition of steadfast and loyal, and I'll take that over being able to leap a tall building in a single bound any day of the week.

Here's the thing: Perry was nine years old when he lost his own dad in a plane crash. That's a tender age to lose one of the most important people in your life, and, by all accounts, his dad was great, full of life and love with a huge thirst for adventure and fun. Perry was left with a void where there once was a dad. I mean, sure, he had the lessons and love that his father had instilled in his first nine years, but now what?

I'll tell you what. Men in the community stepped up to fill in the gap. They made sure my husband continued to learn everything it means to be a man. They took him hunting and fishing, they taught him to look someone in the eye and give a firm handshake, they imparted the value of what it means to give your word and mean it, and they taught him the importance of standing up for what you believe in. They modeled love and loyalty to their families and included my husband in trips and activities where he could find adventure and face challenges. All these years later, he'll tell stories at dinnertime—as we all sit around with our steak knives—about something Jim Martin said, or the time Mr. Holzhausen did that, or how Mr. Swank taught him to do this.

Two weeks after Perry lost his dad, his mom sent him off to summer camp as planned in an attempt to keep life as normal as possible. While he was at camp, he got hurt and ended up in the camp infirmary. As the young camp nurse bandaged him up, she tried to distract him by making conversation and asked, "So what does your dad do?" and Perry answered matter-of-factly, "My dad died two weeks ago." I think we can all safely assume that poor camp nurse is still in therapy over that exchange. But it was an early indicator of how Perry took one of the worst possible things that could happen and chose to never feel sorry for himself. He will say to this day that he never felt cheated because he was surrounded by so many wonderful men in the community who stepped up to the plate.

The thing about dads is, sometimes it's hard to know exactly what they do until they aren't there to do it anymore. Their value is almost an intangible thing because the moms are often the ones who read the bedtime stories and pack the lunches and kiss the skinned knees, but the world needs good dads, and that person needs to be so much more than just someone who contributed their DNA. To me, the real heroes aren't just the dads who love their own families, but who also pour themselves out in the life of kids who need someone in their lives who realizes the importance of having your own steak knife at the dinner table. I watch the way Perry effortlessly knows how to love and equip and challenge Caroline to be the very best version of herself, to make sure she's ready to fly, and I am forever grateful to the men who showed up in Perry's life because they helped him become the man and father he is today—and we wouldn't trade him for anything in the world.

* * *

I met Gulley a long, *long* time ago, when we were both students at Texas A&M. In fact, I accidentally did math the other day and realized we have now been friends for thirty years. That's a whole lot of life lived with each other, and it's safe to say we have seen each other at our very best and at our very worst. Gulley grew up in Bryan, Texas, which is the small town right next to College Station where Texas A&M is located. I don't know why this just turned into a geography lesson, but the cities are so close that the locals refer to the whole area as B/CS.

Anyway, because her whole family lived in Bryan, we spent a lot of time with them while we were students at A&M. You know what college kids love more than just about anything? Besides cheap beer? A place to eat a delicious home-cooked meal and access a washer and dryer to do laundry without stockpiling quarters for weeks on end. In fact, there may have even been a summer when I just moved into her parents' house because it seemed to make more sense than driving over there every single day. And I think it speaks volumes about the kind of people they are, because they let me. And they fed me. And they took me in and made me their own.

Or maybe the whole thing was like the movie, *What About Bob?* But I choose not to examine that too closely.

The thing is, I love them all dearly. They became my second family. At family functions, I'd sit next to Gulley's grandmother, Nena, and we'd often discuss obituaries. I'm not really sure how it happened, but it seems to be a popular topic among the senior set. She told me she has a friend who is a former beauty queen, and she's been writing her own obituary for years because she doesn't feel like anyone else will do her justice. Apparently, she occasionally calls Nena and reads her the latest version of the obituary. Because that is totally normal.

I remember Nena leaned in and whispered to me, "Oh, she goes on and on about how she was a drum majorette and a former Miss Fort Worth County, and a Kappa Alpha Sweetheart Queen, and the homecoming queen at her high school. But she never mentions *a word* about how she's been married *five times*."

In all fairness, that's a lot to work in to one obituary.

The point is, I was a girl in search of family, and I found it. My five years of college—yes, five, because I redshirted my freshman year. What does that mean? I don't really know; I just know it didn't count because I was still dating my high school boyfriend and didn't maximize my college fun and frivolity potential. Anyway, my college years were a time in which I was more than a little lost. My mom had gotten remarried and moved far away, I was in constant dating turmoil, and I'd wandered far away from any semblance of a relationship with God. When I look back on those years, I have a lot of regrets, but most of all, my heart just breaks for the girl I was then. I was so desperate to feel loved and to find my place in the world. Gulley's family became an anchor for me when I was basically lost at sea.

Her parents, to whom we now refer by their grandparent names, Honey and Big, were branches that supported me as I made the climb to see what Jesus looked like and how he loved me. It wasn't necessarily anything they said or did; it was how they loved and lived. Even all these years later, I know their house is a place where I can walk through the door and find Honey has made my favorite brownies (and will make sure I get all the brownie edges because they're my favorite).

All those years ago, I thought I'd found a new best friend and a place to do my laundry, but God knew he'd led me to so much more. He gave me a family and a home. He knew I needed the gift of feeling like I belonged, and he led me through the door of a family who happened to specialize in making everyone around them feel loved and seen. Over the years, I've had a lot of people who served as branches that helped me climb, but they were the first who made me feel secure enough to begin the journey.

✳ ✳ ✳

One of the things I've learned over the years is that the best way to love another is to figure out what that person needs and then find a way to help fill that gap, just the way those men helped fill what would have been a void in Perry's life. No one can be everything to another person, but we can be something. For me, this means asking myself, "How can I live in a way that shows the world a glimpse of Jesus?" Maybe you're reading this and still working out your faith, what and who you believe in, and that's okay. No matter where we are in life, there are universal truths about how to treat others and how to walk this dusty earth in a way that will cause the fewest regrets about how we loved the people around us.

In Luke 19, we read about Zacchaeus, the chief tax collector in Jericho. He knew Jesus was passing through his town and was desperate to see him for himself. And so this hardened tax collector, who also happened to be small in stature, didn't hesitate to climb a sycamore tree to get a better view of this Jesus he'd heard about. Here's the question: how can we be the tree in someone's life? How can we be the embodiment of what allows the world to get a better view of Jesus? We are surrounded by people who are hurting, broken, lonely, and lost; people who have climbed all the wrong trees in search of something to give their lives meaning and purpose. How can we live in a way that answers a lot of their questions? Are the branches of our life kindness, humility, love, acceptance, joy, and peace? People don't care about our statement of faith; they care about our actions. "Who is wise and understanding among you?" asks James. "Let them show it by their good life, by deeds done in the humility that comes from wisdom" (James 3:13). I don't want to hear about how great your tree is if you can't show me that it bears fruit.

I have a dear friend named Nancy who raised her kids, lost one of them to suicide, survived that heartache, and now has a bunch of darling grandbabies. We met several years ago, and while we haven't spent much time together in person, we have a strong connection with each other. Every now and then, she'll text me something like, "You're on my mind and in my prayers. Always, but especially this week. May God be so glorified through all you do! I'm so for you! Much love to you!" There is never a day when I get a text from her that I didn't need that encouragement or the assurance that someone is praying for me, and I know I'm not the only one she prays for and encourages in this way. I don't know how Nancy learned to love so well, but

I know she's taught me how to better love and encourage the people around me.

It's not always easy. A lot of times, love looks like being the thing in someone else's life that you felt was missing from your own. When you recognize that emptiness in another person, it's because it's the very same emptiness you've felt. That's the redemptive power of loving the people around us.

Here's the bright side: it's in the pouring out of ourselves by loving others that we ultimately find who we were created to be.

CHAPTER 12

THE BRIGHT SIDE OF LIFE GIVING YOU LEMONS

I hate the character-building weeks.
They are THE WORST.

—MELANIE SHANKLE

Pat and Leslie are dear friends of ours who recently sold their house in the city and moved to the outskirts of San Antonio to build a custom home on a little bit of land because it had always been their dream. This meant they spent over a year living in an apartment with their three young kids, and let's be honest, by the time the house was finished, their vision may have changed to "any place that doesn't require us to climb up a flight of stairs with three kids and fifty bags of groceries."

Leslie has a great eye for design. She's not an interior decorator by trade, but she's the person you want helping you if you have a creative project, because her style is impeccable. True story: My best friend, Gulley, and I both met Leslie separately years ago, and kept telling each other about this mom in the neighborhood who wore funky hats to soccer games and always dressed in a way that didn't look like anyone else. Obviously, we both adored her, and then ultimately realized we were talking about the same person because it's a small community and there are only so many Leslies who wear fedoras and motorcycle boots to soccer games—like probably six or seven, tops.

So Leslie and her husband, Pat, spent over a year painstakingly planning and poring over every little detail of their new home. They picked out tile, light fixtures, flooring, all those things you have to pick out when you're building a home from the ground up. Just the thought of it puts me square on the edge of a panic attack because we renovated our house years ago, and

I thought I was equipped to handle big life decisions until the electrician asked me where we'd like our light switches, and the pressure was too much. Light switches anywhere I want them? Madness. That's when I learned I need someone to just put in some light switches and not give me any choice in the matter. (By the way, the electrician insisted I make the decision, and I am sad to tell you that even fifteen years later, I am reminded every day that I chose poorly.)

Finally, the day arrived for them to move their family into the new house. And we all know that isn't a day-long process. It's weeks of figuring out where you want the couch and does the TV really look best there? It's wondering why you have so much stuff for your kitchen and how you accumulated so many knick-knacks and why your kids are always saying they're bored when they clearly have an overabundance of possessions. But, finally, about a month after the original move-in date, the house had turned into a home. Everything was where they wanted it, the boxes were mercifully cleared away, and they could go back to the business of functioning as a normal family in their beautiful, new home after being crammed in a small apartment for a year.

It was about a week into this new normalcy that Pat and Leslie settled on the couch one night to watch TV. Their three kids were all in bed, so it was that time of day when you can actually unwind and relax and say a prayer that all the children stay in their beds because you might lose your mind if one of them pops up to ask for a seventy-fifth glass of water. As they put their feet up on the coffee table and got ready to watch a basketball game together, there was suddenly a weird noise from behind them, and the next thing they knew, a smelly, dirty, wet cat jumped right in between them on the couch.

Here's the first problem: They don't own a cat.

Here's the second problem: The cat immediately jumped off the couch and began to race around the house. This smelly, dirty, wet cat was on the loose in their beautiful new home and, even worse, he was heading straight for the kids' bedrooms. And there is no tragedy like a tragedy that involves the possibility of waking sleeping children. They didn't have time to figure out from whence the cat came because the immediate problem was how to get him out of their house while not waking up the kids.

Pat grabbed a broom as his cat-removal device of choice. They began opening doors and windows, trying to get the cat to run outside. But the cat was on a mission of terror. He ran into their middle child's bedroom, perched right on top of their son's head, and hissed at them. They shooed him out of that room and tried to get him to the closest exit, but the cat detoured into the youngest child's room and leapt from corner to corner, dodging their attempts to get him out and ending up in the closet, where he managed to rub his dirty, wet, smelly cat body on every article of clothing in there. And while all of this was going on, they began to notice exactly how bad the feline intruder smelled. Everything he came in contact with reeked of evil and poop. He was leaving dirty, wet footprints all over everything he touched: the floor, the bedding, the custom-made curtains that he decided to swing from momentarily.

Finally, Leslie was able to block his path while Pat corralled him down the entryway and out the front door. They shut all the doors and windows and then just looked at each other as they took a few deep breaths, incredulously wondering, WHAT ON EARTH JUST HAPPENED? It's one of those moments when you wonder if you just hallucinated or was there really a dirty, wet, smelly cat just rampaging through the house? Just a typical, everyday scenario.

They checked on the kids, who had all mercifully slept through the entire scene, then did their best to clean up the mess and get rid of the smell. And then Pat and Leslie began to research the issue of where the cat had originated from, other than hell. The doors and windows had all been closed. No one had used the front door or even gone in or out since much earlier in the evening. Then Pat walked back to check the entrance from the garage into the house and that's when he realized what must have happened to that poor cat.

The door from the garage leads directly into a mudroom where they put an extra refrigerator for cold drinks and normal fridge overflow. The door to the bonus refrigerator was wide open, and the inside of it looked like a crime scene, covered in all manner of cat hair and cat bodily fluids and, well, just picture your worst nightmare because that was the inside of the refrigerator. It was a scene from a horror movie that you never wanted to see and will now haunt you for the rest of your life.

There are many things about what exactly happened to the cat that will remain solely between the cat and God. But using their best deductive reasoning skills, Pat and Leslie determined that the cat must have gotten into the house while Leslie was bringing in groceries from the car earlier that morning. She was loading soft drinks directly into the mudroom refrigerator, and left the refrigerator door open while she went back and forth from the car to the fridge. At some point, she finished the job and closed the refrigerator door. This was all fine and good, except for the fact that the cat had decided to get inside the refrigerator. Here are some questions you may have:

1. *Why did the cat get in the refrigerator?* Look. I don't know this cat's life. But I do know it was the middle of summer in South Texas, and I have had moments myself when it seemed reasonable and life-giving to consider curling up in the middle of a refrigerator and taking a nap.

2. *How did Leslie not notice there was a cat in the refrigerator when she closed the door?* If you are asking this question, then you've clearly never unloaded a car full of groceries in the summer heat with three small children underfoot. She's not even sure she's the one who shut the refrigerator door, but you hate to blame your children for everything. They take enough heat for all the sleep deprivation they cause and how they make all your money disappear.

It would seem that the hero of this story, the dirty, smelly, wet cat, discovered he was in more than a little bit of a pickle and spent many hours valiantly trying to escape from the inside of the refrigerator, and in what has to be definitive proof that cats do indeed have nine lives, he succeeded in freeing himself from his chilly prison. He then rejoiced in his ninja-like feat by jumping right between Pat and Leslie as they sat on the couch before wreaking havoc on their spotless new home in a show of vengeance and justice. They have not seen the cat since he ran out their front door that evening, and I think it's safe to say he never will venture into their house or even their yard ever again. Chill me once, shame on you. Chill me twice, shame on me.

But here's what I thought about after I laughed until I cried when I first heard this story: isn't it just the way life sometimes goes? Just when we think we can relax and let our guard down, just when we take a deep breath and pour a glass of wine to celebrate, life drops a dirty, wet, smelly cat right on our couch. We didn't see the cat coming. We planned for lots of different scenarios and dreamed a lot of dreams, and none of them involved a cat that escaped from our refrigerator. One minute everything seems like maybe it's going according to plan, and then the next minute we're in the midst of chaos, trying to get a dirty, wet cat out of our house and our lives.

✳ ✳ ✳

Almost ten years ago, my dear friend Meredith's dad was hit by a car while he was out walking the dog early one morning. It was a hit-and-run, and Meredith's mom only knew something was amiss when their dog showed up at the house by itself. They found her dad moments later, and he was rushed to the hospital. They were able to save his life, although he was never the same, and he ultimately passed away a little less than two years later.

I met Meredith during my first senior year of college. She and Gulley had become friends through a series of events that, I think, involved dating boys who happened to be friends. I immediately liked Meredith. She's hard not to like because she is hilarious, and that happens to be one of my favorite personality traits in a person. But she's also kind, loyal, and doesn't mind letting you borrow her clothes, which was a trait I valued immensely in my college years.

We ended up living together during my last year of college, along with Gulley and our other friend, Paige. I soon learned that Mer came from a close-knit family, and to gain Mer as a friend was to also gain her parents and her younger brother. They were a package deal, and I adored them. Her parents both worked in education for years, and her dad was a school superintendent, and maybe that explains why they had the ability to make us all feel like they were always on our side and interested in our lives. Chris and Eddie made the trek to College Station from their home in Kilgore, Texas, for every single Texas A&M home game and always spent time at the little duplex where we lived, catching up with us and giving us good advice. To this day, I still use my ring finger to gently apply makeup and moisturizer around my eyes because Chris told us that the skin around your eyes is very delicate and you want to avoid pulling it and causing wrinkles. But I think the thing that stood out most to me about Chris and Eddie Little was the way they loved each other. Maybe it's because I grew up with parents who divorced, but I always noticed the genuine affection they had for each other, even after all those years of marriage and having two almost-grown children.

Over the ensuing years, I'd see them from time to time when one of us got married or happened to be at an Aggie game, and of course, I kept in regular contact with Meredith. I knew that her dad had decided to retire so they could move closer now that Meredith was married and the mother of two little girls. Whenever I'd talk to Mer, she'd laugh about how "BeBe" loved her girls, and how his job was to get them to school every morning. He was teaching the girls to play golf and fully embracing his role as grandfather. She told me her parents were loving retirement and planning to do some traveling and see the world together.

That's why it came as such a shock the day Mer called to tell us about the accident. Her dad had always been so vibrant and full of life in a way that belied his age. Her parents had plans and dreams that they had yet to fulfill, and all that was cut short in one devastating instant. Over the next two years, instead of traveling and playing golf and enjoying retirement, Chris became Eddie's caretaker. They had to figure out how to maneuver a world of insurance billing, hospitals, rehabilitation, home health care, and a thousand other logistics you never think about until your world changes. Life changed in a moment. This was not what any of them planned for; it was millions of miles away from where they expected to be.

Eventually, all the health complications from the accident took the ultimate toll, and Eddie passed away, leaving behind a wife who loved him dearly, two kids who still miss him every day, and two granddaughters who thought he hung the moon. Sometimes the dirty, wet, smelly cat in your life is a lot worse than a dirty, wet, smelly cat, and none of us are immune to those moments, no matter our spiritual depth, socioeconomic status, or family situation.

Here's the thing, in case you haven't figured this out already: life doesn't always go the way we plan. Or, as I like to call it, "Tuesday." And most of us love a plan. Our plan is like the ring in *The Lord of the Rings*; it's our precious. We hold it closely, we cherish it, and maybe we even idolize it a little bit. Why else does a job called life coach actually exist? We like to set goals and then map out how we are going to achieve them. It gives us this great illusion that we are in control. We love control. Control is safe. Control is our friend.

The reality is, even if you don't have a formal, written life plan, you have a life plan in your head. We all do. You have an imagined future. You may want to fall in love, start a family, have kids, get a college degree, build a business, travel to Europe, rock grandbabies on the front porch, or watch all fifteen seasons of *Grey's Anatomy*. We want to attain a certain level of comfort and stability for ourselves. We want our life to actually mean something. We don't want to waste it, and so we plan.

Plans are good. There is not one thing wrong with making a plan. Without plans, we'd probably get very little accomplished. Those who fail to plan often find themselves binge-watching Netflix. Ask me how I know. Yet there are many times when God intentionally messes up our plans. And by "many times," I mean a whole lot of the time. There are also the times when life is just messy and complicated because this space of time between the beginning and the end isn't for the faint of heart. We have all had or will have those seasons that seem impossible to make it through, when the darkness seems to eclipse the light and leaves us feeling lost and helpless and totally out of control. So much of who we will become and how God can use our lives depends on our response. Maybe the very thing that feels like it will destroy us is the thing that brings God near to us. Take it from Joseph.

We meet Joseph in Genesis 37. He was his father's favorite son to the point that his dad, Jacob, made him a coat of many colors. Maybe you recall this from both Sunday school lessons and the Dolly Parton song. Joseph was the only one of his brothers who was bestowed a gift as meaningful as a couture coat. Not only that, Joseph had a dream in which he saw sheaves of wheat that represented his brothers bowing down to him, and then he had a dream where the stars were his brothers and bowed down to him.

Needless to say, his brothers didn't really receive this well. Pro tip: If you're the pampered, spoiled younger brother with a fabulous coat that your brothers already resent, maybe don't share at the dinner table about your dreams that involve them bowing down to you.

For all his naivete about how to win friends and influence people, Joseph dreamed of being a leader, and he dreamed of making a difference. But like all dreamers, he was surrounded by detractors who didn't understand, and his dream became too much for them. So his brothers plotted to kill him. When Joseph was seventeen years old, they threw him into a pit and left him for dead, and he was then sold into slavery. But God never left Joseph, and over the next twenty years, in spite of the obstacles in his way and the challenges he would face, including false accusations and imprisonment, Joseph rose to the second-highest position in all of Egypt and ended up saving the very brothers who had betrayed him from famine and starvation, along with the entire nation of Israel. Joseph ultimately lived to see God fulfill the dreams he'd had all those years before, but it included a journey he never could have imagined. It was a journey more tear-filled and volatile than the most dramatic rose ceremony ever on *The Bachelor*. In the end, his brothers did end up bowing before him in fear and trembling because Joseph had the power to end their lives. Yet everything Joseph had experienced—the heartache, the injustice, the betrayal, the hurt, the loss—had caused his faith and trust in God to grow and given him a perspective and a wisdom he never would have had otherwise.

✳ ✳ ✳

If you had asked me the summer before Caroline's sophomore year of high school if she had close girlfriends, I would have said unequivocally, yes. I felt fortunate that she had seemingly dodged the mean girl bullet for the most part and found a group of friends who appeared to be fairly drama-free. But it turns out I had exhaled too soon because, just a few weeks later, the beginning of the school year brought a level of meanness, back-stabbing, and manipulation that would cause Regina George from *Mean Girls* to say, "Wow, that's a little harsh." I began to dread the moment I picked her up from school every day because I never knew what she might have had to deal with over the course of the eight hours she spent there. I suddenly understood why people switch their child to another school or homeschool them instead of sending them to a place where they will return to you emotionally wrung out. This wasn't something I had envisioned being part of her high school experience, because Caroline is a level-headed kid and has always had such a good sense of who she is and what she wants out of life. She prizes loyalty, honesty, and kindness, and pours out those qualities in abundance on the people she loves and cares about. But these girls, who had been her closest friends, had turned on her for reasons I don't think I'll ever fully understand except to surmise that they were rooted in feeling insecure and insignificant and somehow, turning on another girl gave them some imitation of whatever they were hoping to find.

As a mom, I don't know that there is anything harder than to watch your child fight a battle you can't do anything about. I couldn't fix this. I could talk through it with her; I could make a bubble bath for her to soak in at the end of another long, hard day; I could pray with her; I could try to make her laugh and remember that life wouldn't always be this way. I could point out examples from my past about how no one wants to peak in high school. I couldn't stop the arrows that were being aimed at her every day, but I prayed like crazy that God's voice would speak to her louder than any others, reminding her that she is loved, treasured, and valued more than she can imagine. There were mornings I'd pray with her as I drove her to school and then give her a pep talk along the lines of, "Keep a smile on your face and stay strong. You will get through this. You have people who love and adore you, and don't ever forget that," then she'd get out of the car, and I'd watch her shift her backpack over her shoulder and take a deep breath as she prepared to face whatever was about to come her way, and I would do my best to make it out of the car drop-off line before I cried all the way home.

This wasn't the way it was supposed to be. Yet it's exactly where we found ourselves.

Life can be hard when the people who are supposed to be our safe places are incapable of loving us the way we hope to be loved. The wounds caused by our families and friends can cut the deepest because they are the ones we should be able to rely on. All of us have watched enough episodes of *This Is Us* to wish our family looked like the Pearson family, except for maybe the part about Jack dying when the Crock-Pot malfunctioned and set the house on fire. All of us have been betrayed by a friend at some point and wished for a group that acted more like Ross, Monica, Chandler, Joey, and Rachel.

All it takes to stop the dysfunction is for one brave person to ask God for the strength and determination to change the narrative, but you have to allow God to heal the parts of you that are still raw and wounded, or you will carry that baggage and your insecurities into the new thing you're asking God to create. He will give you beauty for ashes always, but it can take time, and it requires standing strong for what you know to be true. And there will be people who won't like or appreciate the stand you are taking to build a healthier future or your decision to walk away.

Sometimes, faithfulness to God sets us on a course where circumstances seem to get worse, not better. That's when we have to dig deep and choose to believe that God is always good even when our lives are hard. It's our faith in the nature of God that will sustain us in those lonely, desperate moments when we don't understand why life is falling apart. Ultimately, faith is believing that God always does what he says he will do, but realizing that rarely ever looks the way we thought it would. Psalm 46:10 says, "Be still, and know that I am God." The original Hebrew translation of "be still" doesn't mean be quiet or don't move; it means let go. Those are very different things. Let go and know that I am God. Let go of trying to control everything. Let go of worry. Let go of unforgiveness, let go of your past, let go of what you can't control and trust that God is in control. His silence doesn't mean he isn't working.

The apostle Peter writes, "Dear friends, do not be surprised at the fiery ordeal that has come on you to test you, as though something strange were happening to you. But rejoice inasmuch as you participate in the sufferings of Christ, so that you may be overjoyed when his glory is revealed" (1 Peter 4:12–13).

So that sounds fun. Don't we all wish for more "fiery ordeals" in our life? Just yesterday I thought, "Man, today is boring. Where is a fiery ordeal for me to handle?" But let's read the verse through to the end. We will be "overjoyed when his glory is revealed." There is always light at the end of the tunnel, and that light will far outshine whatever we are going through now. No dark season lasts forever.

Joseph was sold into slavery, spent many of the ensuing years in an Egyptian prison, was left alone and abandoned, but he continued to trust in God. Over and over again, as we read his story in Genesis, we see phrases such as these:

"The LORD was with Joseph so that he prospered . . ." (Genesis 39:2).

". . . his master saw that the LORD was with him and that the LORD gave him success in everything he did . . ." (Genesis 39:3).

". . . the LORD blessed the household of the Egyptian because of Joseph. The blessing of the LORD was on everything Potiphar had . . ." (Genesis 39:5).

". . . while Joseph was there in the prison, the LORD was with him . . ." (Genesis 39:20–21).

And we can look at that and be like, "Yeah, he was in *prison*. No thank you." But God had a plan that went way beyond Joseph's circumstances. Likewise, God has plans for us that go way beyond our momentary circumstances.

We are not victims. When we choose to walk around feeling sorry for ourselves, we are discounting the very nature of God, his goodness, and his faithfulness. Nobody can stop what God wants to do in your life but you. The apostle Paul writes, "But we have this treasure in jars of clay to show that this all-surpassing power is from God and not from us. We are hard pressed on every side, but not crushed; perplexed, but not in despair; persecuted, but not abandoned; struck down, but not destroyed" (2 Corinthians 4:7–9).

God knows we are flawed and cracked and far from perfect, but it's those very cracks in our armor of self-protection and frailty that allow his light to shine through us. We will never really know ourselves or our God until we have been tested by adversity and hard times.

It's who we become in the messy parts of the waiting and the living and the worst moments that we never wanted or asked for that determine if we will be the people he created us to be. Often, everything we've put our faith in which is not God has to be burned to the ground in order for something new to grow.

Writing what he has heard from God, the prophet Isaiah states:

> I will lead the blind by ways they have not known,
>> along unfamiliar paths I will guide them;
> I will turn the darkness into light before them
>> and make the rough places smooth. (Isaiah 42:16)

As you walk into places in your life that are unfamiliar, trust him to guide you through the dark places and to make the rough places smooth.

Everything we need—in our marriages, our jobs, our kids, our friends, our hard times and our disappointments—we already possess in Christ because he is the source of all hope and strength. And just because there are times when nothing looks the way we thought it would doesn't mean God isn't working all those things together for our ultimate good. We just don't have the perspective he has—we can't see the whole, infinite picture.

At the end of Joseph's story, after he has saved the land from famine, his brothers come to him, throw themselves down before him, and say, "We are your slaves." Joseph says to them, "Don't be afraid. Am I in the place of God? You intended to harm me, but God intended it for good to accomplish what is now being done, the saving of many lives" (Genesis 50:18–20).

Joseph had been through hell and back at the hands of his

own family, yet he recognized that he had fulfilled the purpose God had for his life, even though it didn't look the way he'd thought it would. He trusted God enough to forgive the ones who had caused so much pain.

In the midst of all the friend drama Caroline was going through, God was faithful to surround her with people who supported her and loved her. As hard as it was, I couldn't deny the way God was using it to shape her faith and make her stronger than she had been before. And she has come out on the other side of it with friends who know how to build each other up and who realize they don't have to drag someone else down to make themselves feel better. As painful as it can be to watch the moments that become cornerstones of character, there is no doubt that we need those very experiences to make us into better versions of who we were before and to appreciate the good things that come into our lives after a season of loss and hurt.

God is a God of cleaning up messes, both the ones we make with our own two hands and the ones that are the dirty, wet, smelly cats that get dropped into our lives. Sometimes we feel like we are helpless and wonder how much more we can take, but God is always there, and he will use these hard things in our lives if we allow him to work. The tears, the heartache, the sleepless nights, the grief—trust him with those.

During that season of watching Caroline struggle and deal with hard situations, I didn't always know what to say. I prayed that God would give me wisdom, and one night, when we were in the middle of a long talk, I told her (please hear this in a voice that befits a Lifetime movie monologue), "Remember, the rarest orchid blooms in adversity." She looked right at me and asked, "Is that from *Mulan*? Did you just quote *Mulan* to me?"

Um. Yes.

It seemed I basically had.

But in my defense, Caroline had only herself to blame because she made me watch it with her 5,076 times from the time she was three years old until she was eight. So I realized I might be better off turning to the Bible for wisdom as opposed to a Disney movie and came across this gem:

> But blessed is the one who trusts in the LORD,
>> whose confidence is in him.
> They will be like a tree planted by the water
>> that sends out its roots by the stream.
> It does not fear when heat comes;
>> its leaves are always green.
> It has no worries in a year of drought
>> and never fails to bear fruit. (Jeremiah 17:7–8)

These verses don't say that a tree planted by the water won't experience drought or heat, because it will. But when its roots are deep, it will never fail to bear fruit or have green leaves in spite of those things.

When our trust is in God, we are like that tree. Drought will come, heat will blaze overhead, hard times will happen, marriages will fail, bad diagnoses will come, accidents will happen, friends will hurt us, and the things we thought we could plan on may never come to pass. Yet when we sink our roots deep into the love God has for us, we will come out stronger and wiser on the other side.

And better equipped to handle all the dirty, wet, smelly cats that may lie ahead.

Here's what I know: there may be a time when you will face a loss so great that your heart will never be the same. Why do bad things happen? Because life happens, and it is ultimately the greatest mystery wrapped in adventure and fraught with danger and full of both joy and heartache.

The bright side is that you have a God who is always working for your good, even in the hardest of times.

CHAPTER 13

THE BRIGHT SIDE OF
MAKING DECISIONS

*Every time you make a choice you
are turning the central part of you,
the part of you that chooses, into
something a little different from what
it was before . . . you are slowly turning
this central thing either into a heavenly
creature or a hellish creature.*

—C.S. LEWIS, *MERE CHRISTIANITY*

Gulley and I were college students at Texas A&M back in the early 1990s. This probably doesn't mean anything to you if you aren't familiar with Texas A&M, but what it means to those who know Aggie history is that we were students during some golden years of football. The Aggies never lost a home game during my entire time as a student, and this meant the team usually played in the Cotton Bowl on New Year's Day. My group of friends and I were never ones to miss any sort of football extravaganza, especially when it meant spending New Year's Eve in Dallas, where there are plenty of good times to be had.

During my senior year of college, we once again made the New Year's trek to Dallas to watch the Aggies play. This was also the year Gulley ruined a pair of gorgeous Nine West suede booties she had bought right before Christmas. We somehow ended up walking through mud during our New Year's Eve festivities and then an ill-advised number of tequila shots led us to believe that washing her new suede boot shoes in the hotel sink was a good idea. (Insert narrator voice here, saying IT WAS NOT A GOOD IDEA.) Looking back, I guess the boot shoe incident was Bad Decision #1. Actually, maybe the tequila shots were Bad Decision #1 and the boot shoes were Bad Decision #2. But we were twenty-one years old and had less common sense than housecats.

Anyway, by the time we got to the actual football game on New Year's Day, we had only enough money left to buy one hot dog, which four or five of us had to share by passing it down the line and each taking one bite. We were freezing cold, hungover from the aforementioned tequila shots, and starving. College students know how to have a good time but often lack the skills to comprehend the consequences of dumb behavior. Gulley and I had plans to catch a flight to Oklahoma right after the football game was over, to visit my mom, so we had a friend drop us off at the airport later that afternoon. The problem was, the weather had turned cold and icy, and all flights were being cancelled. We found this out after we had boarded our flight and then been asked to deboard and make our way back to the terminal.

So we were stranded with no money and even less sense. We were tired and cold and basically a hair shy of feeling like the Ingalls family during a Minnesota winter. The voice on the intercom was directing everyone to get in line at the various airport counters to make arrangements for different flight options. Since this was in the days before the internet, we had no choice but to get in a long line and wait while time stood still at the American Airlines counter. It was while we were in this long line that we began to strike up conversations with our fellow stranded travelers, all of whom were throwing out different travel strategies that wouldn't involve spending the night sleeping and drooling in a hard plastic airport chair using our luggage as a pillow. One older man in line right in front of us (I say older, but looking back, he was probably forty) decided he was going to try his luck at the rental car counter. He had been on the same flight to Oklahoma we were on, so we knew our destinations were the same. When he came back to find us in line about thirty minutes later, announced that he had procured a rental car, and offered to let us ride with him to Oklahoma, Gulley and I looked at each other briefly as if to mentally calculate all the Lifetime movies we had seen that suggested this might be a bad idea before we grabbed our bags and followed him out of the airport. This is essentially material for the opening scene of *Taken 2* starring Liam Neeson. Oh, and we also stopped at a pay phone and left messages for our parents, letting them know our flight had been cancelled but not to worry because we had hitched a ride with what appeared to be a nice man in the airport who was going to drive us to Oklahoma. What convinced us he was a nice man? We'd seen him carry a Bible onto the plane earlier and decided that serial killers don't carry Bibles. At the time, it seemed like not only an unobjectionable assumption, but a correct one.

Dear Reader, I feel the need to let you know right up front that it all worked out okay, because I can feel that you are waiting to get to the *Dateline NBC* part of this story. But let's all agree right now that the decision to get in a car with a strange man we met in an airport will forever rank as one of the dumbest things I have ever done. We had no cell phones in case this went off the rails and no sort of black belt martial arts training to defend ourselves. We were two incredibly stupid college girls who managed in an instant to age our parents one hundred years with this stupid decision. Even worse, we got in the car with him and, after making a little bit of small talk, fell asleep for the remainder of the trip. Honestly, I have to put my head between my knees to keep from passing out just remembering the vast stupidity of it all. Now that I have a daughter myself, I realize this is basically everything you try to teach your kids not to do. And, maybe worst of all, when our parents were furious with us for being so stupid, we justified the whole thing by sharing with them our theory about serial killers not carrying Bibles.

All of this is to tell you what you have most likely already deduced: I am historically a bad decision maker. Actually, as I've gotten older, it's not the decisions themselves that are terrible so much as it is that I hate deciding things. Now that the Enneagram exists, I know this has a lot to do with me being an Enneagram 9. I just want everyone to be happy, and if I make a decision, then the weight of everyone's happiness rests solely on my shoulders, and that's just entirely too much pressure. True story: part of the reason I probably agreed to ride to Oklahoma with a total stranger thirty years ago was because I didn't want to hurt his feelings by saying no. This is basically how every Lifetime movie starts.

Side note: isn't it weird how the Enneagram thing has just completely taken over? It seems like you can take a class at church to find out your Enneagram type and that there are books and social media solely devoted to what it all means. You know what it reminds me of? Remember in the 1980s how women were super into what season they were? You were either a spring, summer, fall, or winter, and each season had colors that supposedly looked best on you. It was a whole thing, and it's the reason that, to this day, I don't think I can wear pastel colors, yet you never hear anyone talk about it anymore. What I'm saying is, do we think it's possible that the Enneagram is the Color Me Beautiful of this generation? Of course, now I'm rereading this whole paragraph and wondering if maybe Color Me Beautiful was only a big thing in my teen years because I grew up in a small southeast Texas city in a family of women whose hallmark was their vanity. This is a real possibility.

Anyway, decisions. Here's a decision I can make every time: I do not want to eat Chinese food. Ever. No one wishes this wasn't true more than I do. I used to love Chinese food. I loved General Tso and his chicken. But twenty years ago, when Perry and I were newlyweds, we took a busload of kids skiing in Durango, Colorado, over spring break as part of his job with Campus Life Ministries. The last night we were there, we ate Chinese food at a little restaurant in downtown Durango before getting on a bus for the seventeen-hour drive home. As it turns out, the Chinese dinner didn't agree with me. By this, I mean that I was violently ill for fifteen hours of the seventeen-hour trip. On a bus. With high school kids. And my new husband, who wasn't supposed to know I had bodily functions that were less than appealing. Thus, Chinese food of all variations is now dead to me. On the plus side, when I'm in a group of people trying to decide where to go eat dinner, I can always be counted on to pipe in and say, "I'm good with anything except Chinese food." This creates the illusion that I am contributing to the final decision without me having to take total responsibility for the final decision. And this basically tells you everything you need to know about me.

There are decisions that are always easy to make, of course. Gulley and I always say that if you order the shrimp and grits at our neighborhood pool, then you have only yourself to blame when you get food poisoning. It shouldn't require much thought for you to realize that shellfish cooked by teenagers in an un-air-conditioned shack in Texas in July is a recipe for disaster. But the thing about life is, it's filled with numerous fork-in-the-road moments, often with big implications, that will leave you unsure which direction you are supposed to take. And what I've usually found is that most of these things aren't as black-and-white as I'd like them to be; you can have two good options in front of you and still have to choose only one. This is filed in the category of my life known as "Can I Please Just Take a Nap Because It's Making My Head Hurt?"

From the time Caroline was little, I would implore her to "make good choices." This used to be as simple as remembering to share her crayons and be kind to the kids in her preschool class, and to let me know she needed to go to the bathroom before we were in the very middle of H-E-B and my entire cart was filled with groceries. Now I talk to Caroline all the time about the more important decisions she has in front of her: where to go to college, what to major in, whom she will marry, where she will live, what she wants to do with her life. These are the big ones. These are the decisions that most people would agree make up about 98 percent of all your life's happiness or misery. And I can't make those decisions for her; I can only equip her with everything she needs to be able to make those decisions for herself.

Do I have it all figured out? No. But gather 'round the campfire known as Insta-stories, children, while I share what I believe to be a valuable tip on how to make good decisions. I have to share this somewhere because maybe then my own child might think I know what I'm talking about instead of rolling her eyes at me.

Here's the secret to life: put God first. Every good decision I've made can be traced directly back to how much I trusted God and listened to his voice before I made it. This biblical wisdom has always served me well when I apply it:

> Trust in the LORD with all your heart
>> and lean not on your own understanding;
> in all your ways submit to him,
>> and he will make your paths straight. (Proverbs 3:5–6)

The heart of this verse is that you have to have a relationship with God to be able to trust him. If I don't know God or believe he wants what's best for me, then it becomes impossible to rely on him to guide me as I weigh my options. This would be like going to an internet forum to get advice from an "expert." Which, by the way, I have been known to do on several occasions as I google, "How do I stop my dog from having diarrhea?" and immediately believe that rice and chicken broth is the answer because Susan from Kansas City typed it on a forum called "Your Pet Is Your Best Friend." Do I know Susan or her qualifications as a pet dietician? Nope. So why do I trust her? I can't tell you why, because it makes no sense.

Here are a few other questions I try to remember to ask myself before I jump: *How will this affect me? How will it affect the people I love and who love me? What do I really want deep down in my heart? Does it honor God? Does it line up with what I know to be true? Is it biblically sound?*

And here's the other thing I've learned along the way: we won't always make the right choice. We are terribly flawed. It's so easy to get caught up in a moment or a feeling. As humans, we crave that initial adrenaline rush of a new thing or a new challenge or just generally pleasing the people around us. This is how I accidentally said yes to being in charge of selling ads for the sports program at Caroline's high school. It happens. We get carried away. It's also how I found myself engaged to a man who was completely wrong for me when I was twenty-two years old and had to figure out how to end the relationship, which meant causing no small amount of pain to all parties involved.

But God is so gracious, so kind and merciful, beyond what we can comprehend. There is no decision that will ruin us forever.

There is no misstep that disqualifies us from turning our lives around. Sometimes we take a leap of faith that absolutely seems right in the moment, but it turns out we jumped for the wrong ring on the monkey bars and find ourselves with a face full of dirt and blood. That's okay, too. What do we do then? Get up and try again. We aren't defined by our last bad decision; we are defined by the decision we make next. We ask for forgiveness where it's needed, trust God to meet us where we are, and be brave enough to take the next step, face the next challenge, and make a new choice. That's what separates us from the animals. Well, that and our ability to accessorize, according to Clairee Belcher in *Steel Magnolias*.

And, actually, my dog, Piper, just chose to eat a half dozen cupcakes that were sitting on my kitchen island, so while she may not know how to make right choices, she does know how to make good choices.

Here's the bright side: we live in a time when we have so many choices available to us. They cause us to wrestle with things, grow as people, and learn from our mistakes. I'll always take having too many choices over having none at all.

CHAPTER 14

THE BRIGHT SIDE OF
TECHNOLOGY

Netflix is the greatest invention of the twenty-first century.

—MELANIE SHANKLE

The fall after I turned fifteen, I got my very first job that didn't involve babysitting neighborhood kids. Actually, I didn't go out and actively pursue employment opportunities so much as my dad told me that one of his good friends from high school owned a record store right by our house, and he'd asked him if he'd hire me. Some parents write checks for half a million dollars to get their kids into USC, but my dad used his influence to get me a job at Sound Castle records, located in a strip mall on Phelan Boulevard in Beaumont, Texas. These two things are almost the same.

The year was 1986, so I would be making $3.35 an hour, which was minimum wage at the time. Clearly, I was heady with the idea of how rich I would soon be. And for those of you who are under the age of thirty, let me clarify that a record store was an establishment where you could buy albums and/or cassette tapes by your favorite artists. Sound Castle had a wall of bins containing record albums in alphabetical order by artist and a huge wooden table that ran the length of the store filled with cassette tapes. My duties involved making sure all the merchandise stayed in alphabetical order, ringing up customer purchases on the cash register, and vacuuming the store at the close of business each day. Not in my official job description, but what I considered to be of equal importance: giggling and flirting with all the cute boys who walked through the door.

One day, I showed up for my shift wearing my favorite

Swatch watch dress. This detail isn't pertinent to the story, but I just wanted you to know I owned a Swatch watch dress. It was red and zipped up the front and had the Swatch watch emblem embroidered on it. When I wore it, I felt like I was basically Madonna. Anyway, I showed up for work, and the store had been rearranged to make room for—wait for it—a section in the back that now included a VHS video movie rental section. Our town didn't even have a Blockbuster video store yet, so this was like magic. The fact that you could just pick a movie to rent—as long as the actual VHS tape was still behind the display box— and take it home to watch it in the comfort of your home on a VCR was unbelievable. It was practically sorcery. Plus, the Sound Castle owner installed a small TV with a VCR in the shop to help promote video rentals, which meant my co-workers and I could spend our shifts watching whatever movie we chose that day. This was technology beyond anything I had previously experienced. Up until that point in my life, you could only see a movie at the theater until it was gone, then you could wait years hoping it might show up on TV, and then it was never to be seen again. I essentially grew up like I was in an episode of *Dr. Quinn, Medicine Woman*. My fifteen-year-old self could have never dreamed of a day that a person didn't even have to go to a record store to buy the latest music or rent a movie.

About a year later, Blockbuster finally came to town, and that was the beginning of the end for Sound Castle records. I probably spent hours of my life over the ensuing years walking the aisles at Blockbuster with friends or a boyfriend—and eventually even my husband and child—in search of a movie to rent for the evening. Kids today will never know the heartache of seeing the rows of display boxes for a movie you've been dying to see only to discover there are no actual VHS tapes still available. The struggle was real. Frankly, it's a wonder any of us survived.

Let us join hands before the glowing embers of the LED screen on my Samsung sixty-five-inch flat-screen television and discuss the wonders of living in a time such as this. I mean, sure, the world has lost its collective mind in so many ways, but a lot of us only know that because the internet exists and we are on Twitter. I can get a set of steak knives and some wrinkle cream delivered to my front door by tomorrow if I feel so inclined, and I find consolation in that. Are we going to get blown up by North Korea? Perhaps. I'd better get next-day delivery on that white V-neck T-shirt tunic.

Last summer, I decided that one of my goals—other than to see if I could get away with not having to wear a bathing suit all summer long—was to introduce Caroline to the classic movies of my youth. We watched *Pretty in Pink*, *The Breakfast Club*, *Sixteen Candles*, *Some Kind of Wonderful*, and *Ferris Bueller's Day Off.* What would the 1980s have looked like without John Hughes? Not nearly as good, I'll tell you that. Take away the characters and storylines he gave us, and what's left is not much more than a ripped, splatter-painted sweatshirt, acid-washed jeans, and a pair of jelly shoes. The beauty of a summer-long movie marathon is that it's now as easy as pushing a button on my remote control to find just about anything I could possibly want to see. Any TV show, any movie, any song I want to listen to is available all the time. To someone who grew up listening to the radio with a tape recorder next to me so I could hurry up and push Record and Play simultaneously in order to record my favorite song, this is astounding. I have apps on my phone that allow me to play games, read books, figure out the best way to get somewhere, and color by number. I had a relative who spent some time in a mental hospital back in the 1960s, and my grandmother told me that part of this relative's therapy was to have craft time to help them feel calm and centered. This is precisely what the color-by-number app on my phone (and a glass of wine) does for me.

Side note: I was telling my mother-in-law the other day that I'd gone to the doctor and thought it was remarkable that I pretty much get to check all the "No" boxes next to the list of diseases when I fill out the family health history form. "Well, except for mental illness," she replied. Which is true. So thanks, color-by-number app, for helping me cope.

Kids today will never know what it's like to have to write a research report using only microfiche at the library and a set of ten-year-old encyclopedias, thus limiting their topic choices to things that don't fall in the category of current or even recent events. They'll never know that there used to be a time when you might wonder about the best way to remove permanent ink from your favorite shirt or what other TV show that guy from *This Is Us* used to be on, and not be able to ask Google and immediately have a million answers at your fingertips. They won't know the struggle inherent in having your phone conversation privacy limited to how far the coiled cord could reach. They will never know the mix of thrill and dread that comes with just picking up the telephone when you don't know who is calling. Basically, we are all now the Jetsons.

I was curious about other people's opinions on the best, most life-changing advances in technology over the last few decades, so I did some research. Well, it's research as long as you consider research to be asking people on Instagram what they think. And

I do. Don't hate me because of my vast expertise in science and data analysis. Here are the top twenty answers I received. Please note that they are not listed in order of importance, but rather the degree to which I agree with them in my heart.

1. *Amazon Prime.* Yes, Lord. Won't he do it? There is basically nothing you can't order and have it show up like wizardry at your front door in less than twenty-four hours.

2. *Alexa.* Remember how we all wished for a robot after we saw *Rocky IV* and Rocky gave Paulie that robot for his birthday? Or maybe that was just me. Either way, Alexa is our modern-day robot. When even Gulley's parents, Honey and Big, can say, "Alexa, turn off the lights," before they go to bed every night, you know that Alexa has taken over the world. And I'm almost 42 percent sure the Russians aren't using it to spy on us. It's all fine. Everything is fine.

3. *Online grocery shopping and delivery.* This one may be my personal favorite. As a devout introvert, the fact that I can avoid the grocery store and awkward small talk in the aisles is life-changing. I always used to say I didn't mind cooking dinner, I just hated having to shop for groceries. But now I can get groceries delivered. The sad part is, it's caused me to discover I actually don't like cooking dinner, either.

4. *GPS.* Every time I travel to speak at an event, I come to the fresh realization that I would have had to choose a different career if not for Google Maps. There is no way I am smart and savvy enough to both drive and look at a paper map to figure out how to get places. Even with

Siri directing me, I sometimes have to yell, "I don't know north or east, just tell me to turn right or left!"

5. *The internet.* When Perry and I first got married back in 1997, we bought our first computer. It was enormous. But once we got it hooked up to the World Wide Web with a dial-up connection, we were like cavemen around the first fire. "What does it do? How does it work?" "I don't know. Just type in AOL.com and see what happens." Basically, everything good in our lives stems from the invention of the internet. And, also, everything bad. I see you, Twitter. Don't try to act like you don't know I'm talking about you.

6. *Smartphones.* I bought my first iPhone in 2009, and as I walked out of the store, I was completely hypnotized. I slid my finger across the screen, trying out everything in sight and attempting to send text messages that read, "I'm texting you from my new iPhone, suckers," to everyone I knew because I am mature. After years of suffering through the archaic predictive texting on my Motorola Razr and being mocked by people who liked to tell me they had the exact same phone back when they were in high school, I deserved just a small moment of reveling in my newfound technology. I spent most of the night playing with all the different features and searching the App Store to discover such things as receiving information about a weird law from different parts of the world every day. How did I live thirty-eight years without knowing it's illegal to carry a rabid dog in a taxicab in London? Now, thanks to modern technology and people with way too much time on their hands, I can get that kind of useful

information on a daily basis. I do vividly remember that the first time I went to make a phone call using my new iPhone, I had no idea how to do it, which was kind of important since it was *a phone*. Whatever. I figured it out. And it's pretty amazing that we can carry basically every bit of technology we need in a purse.

7. *Botox.* You know those "elevens" you get between your eyebrows as you get older, from all the times you furrow your brow? Our children won't because elevens will soon cease to exist thanks to the modern marvel that is injecting botulism into ourselves. Talk about building a better tomorrow.

8. *Texting.* Have I mentioned I am an introvert? Being able to send someone a text message is the best thing ever. It eliminates unnecessary small talk and gives me the ability to communicate without worrying if I'm catching someone at a bad time. Plus, emojis and GIFs are my emotional currency. There is no better way to express how I really feel than sending a GIF of a monkey passing gas at a dog through a window.

9. *Google.* What do you need to know? Who do you need to find? What is the gross national debt of Romania? What's the title of that song with a lyric that goes, "You're the only one I need"? These are just the basics of what Google can do for you.

10. *Netflix.* I don't want to overstate it, but Netflix is one of the greatest joys of my life. It single-handedly created the term "binge-watch." It knows me well enough to suggest shows I might enjoy based on shows I've previously watched, just like a best friend would. It doesn't judge

me for binging, but rather gives me the option to simply, "Start next episode." It has alleviated the pressure to watch a new TV show when it first debuts, knowing that if it's any good and I decide I want to watch it, Netflix will give me that option later, commercial-free and at my leisure. And Netflix Originals programming? Some of it is so magnificent, you could contend it's what God created on the eighth day. Did I go too far with that? Perhaps.

11. *Blowout bars.* There are times in life when it seems like too much pressure to be responsible for your own hair. But we live in a day when you can go to a place that specializes in the perfect blow-dry and style, and thereby take a big chunk of stress out of your getting ready for a big event routine. God bless America. When our forefathers talked about the pursuit of happiness, this is probably what they had in mind.

12. *Dry shampoo.* It takes me approximately seventeen hours to blow dry and curl my hair. And I also have a theory that the more I wash my hair, the quicker the color that is covering my grays disappears. My hairdresser swears this isn't true, but I'm just reporting what I've seen. All that to say, there are days when all I'm living on is a prayer and dry shampoo.

13. *Caller ID.* The one sadness with Caller ID is that it has eliminated the thrill of calling a boy you like just to hear him say hello and then hanging up. But it has also taken away the internal quagmire of whether you risk missing an important phone call or answering and having to talk to your Aunt Nancy about her latest case of gout.

14. *Keyless car entry.* The other day I had to rent a car that

didn't have keyless entry, and I lost hours of my life searching for the car keys in the bottom of my purse. Stay tuned for the Lifetime movie starring Judith Light that will tell my story.

15. *Back-up sensors and cameras.* From the time I was sixteen years old until I was twenty-two, I drove a Honda CRX. For those of you who don't know, this is a car that had only two front seats and was the size of a roller skate. It makes a Kia Soul look like a charter bus. Yet I still managed to back into countless trash cans, other cars, and light poles. All I'm saying is, back-up sensors and cameras were created with someone like me in mind.

16. *Kindles/e-readers.* It took me a long time to move on from reading a book in paper form. I still like the feeling of holding a real book in my hand, but you can't beat the convenience of being able to immediately download anything you want to read. Especially now that finding an actual bookstore is like spotting a parakeet in the wild.

17. *Salad in a bag.* The fact that this can be a side dish for any meal and all it requires it opening a bag is proof that God is on his throne. I'm so thankful to Dr. Romaine and Professor Arugula for this invention. I realize it may not be as tasty as a fresh salad I cut up and make myself, but until I can afford to hire someone to do that for me, this will do. Pro tip: If you make your own salad dressing using olive oil, apple cider vinegar, lemon juice, and salt and pepper, and then throw in some dried cranberries, you can create the illusion that you've worked really hard on this salad that came from a bag.

18. *Roomba.* For all the women in the 1950s who had to

vacuum their floors while wearing heels and pearls, this Roomba is for you. I am woman, hear me roar. Also, without the Roomba, what would cats on YouTube videos ride?

19. *Spanx.* I realize they aren't going to win any prizes for comfort, but there are times when nothing else will do. I call those times every time I have to wear a dress.

20. *Mapping the human genome.* Someone put this in the comments on my Instagram request and I was like, well sure. So I googled it, and Wikipedia clarified that the Human Genome Project "was an international scientific research project with the goal of determining the sequence of nucleotide base pairs that make up human DNA, and of identifying and mapping all of the genes of the human genome." I included it because that sounds important. But, even more importantly, can you use it to binge watch *The Office*, or does it deliver your groceries to your front door?

When I think of all the advances that have been made just in my lifetime, it causes me to realize there is no limit to what could be next. Eventually, we'll all be able to just think of a movie, and it will instantly play in our brains. I mean, as it is, I can think right now that I might want a pair of leopard print tennis shoes, and an ad for them will show up in my Instagram feed by tonight.

The bright side is, we are surrounded by more and better technology than we could ever have dreamed of. The trick is figuring out how to use it all—or finding a toddler who can show us how.

CHAPTER 15

THE BRIGHT SIDE OF
FIGHTING TO BE
YOUR TRUE SELF

Today you are you! That is truer than true! There is no one alive who is you-er than you!

—DR. SEUSS, *HAPPY BIRTHDAY TO YOU!*

When I was seven years old, I joined our neighborhood swim team, the Westador Ducks. If you were never a part of your neighborhood swim team, then you can't fully appreciate the feeling of sheer pride that comes from wriggling your body into a one-piece Speedo with red and white stripes to represent your neighborhood. I mean, the Westador Ducks represented both the old and new Westador subdivisions, which meant upwards of twenty different blocks of 1970s brick homes and the residents contained therein. Plus, they were at least the seventh best neighborhood swim team amongst a small subset of similar neighborhoods in the northwest section of Houston, Texas. Needless to say, it was like my own personal Summer Olympics of 1978.

Every morning I suited up, wrapped a towel around my neck, and set out on my blue Huffy bike with the floral banana seat for the Cali Clubhouse, where swim practice took place. Let's not discuss what it would take for me to get on a bicycle wearing only my swimsuit these days. In fact, forget I brought it up and caused what can only be a jarring mental picture.

Once I arrived at practice, I smeared a white stripe of zinc on my nose, put on my goggles, and swam lap after lap, dreaming of the day I'd be as cool as the teenage lifeguards who supervised us as we honed our butterfly, breast, freestyle, and backstroke skills before relaxing poolside afterward with a bag of Doritos and a Dr Pepper from the vending machine. As it turns out, I was a natural at both the butterfly stroke and eating Doritos.

I couldn't wait for our first swim meet to show off my skills, and by the time that first summer was over, I had a whole bulletin board full of ribbons to show for my efforts. I felt levels of accomplishment that I'm not sure I've felt since. There is really nothing as heady or rewarding as the first taste of independence and finding something you're good at, and the Westador Ducks provided me with both of those things.

When the following summer rolled around, I was eager to resume my swimming career. Once again, I had the sweet Speedo one-piece swimsuit with the crisscrossed back that left tan lines that were a source of pride and triumph because they let everyone at the pool know I was on the neighborhood swim team. *No, Cindy, I'm not just your average deadbeat neighborhood kid loitering around, playing freeze tag in Mr. Cashman's yard. Do you see these striped tan lines on my back? I've had my name in the Westador newsletter for finishing first in my heat in the fifty-meter butterfly. I am going places.*

But that summer, I'd moved up to a new age bracket. The competition was tougher. My ribbons went from first and second place to fifth and sixth place. Not even the little boxes of powdered Jell-O mix our coaches let us eat in between races to give us a sugar rush made me feel better about it. (Hello, 1970s, let's feed the children powder made of synthetic ingredients and tons of sugar to prepare them for their athletic endeavors.)

One night, I finally broke down and told my parents how discouraged I was about swim team. I wasn't any good at it anymore. I wasn't fast enough, and my beach towel had gotten caught in the spokes of my bicycle tire on the way to practice one morning, and I could've been killed. Essentially, it was a soliloquy only an eight-year-old girl who wants to quit something could deliver, full of angst and sorrow at what could have been and all the ways life wasn't working out for me. My parents, to their credit, encouraged me to keep going and told me that I just needed to keep working hard and it would pay off. And in that moment, I listened to them. In fact, their response left me feeling so sure of myself that after agreeing I would keep swimming, I let out an ecstatic, "Nothing can stop me now!"

I believe I had seen a character say that exact same line on an *ABC Afterschool Special* called, "It's a Mile from Here to Glory," and felt appropriately inspired. Thus, I'd been looking for an opportunity to make that declaration my own. Because in the seventies and eighties, there was no greater molder of young minds than a powerful *ABC Afterschool Special*—except for maybe that "Very Special Episode" of *Family Ties*, wherein Uncle Ned, played by a young Tom Hanks, turns out to be alcoholic, which we learn by watching him drink a bottle of vanilla extract from the Keatons' pantry.

Anyway, with my plagiarized yet passionate, "Nothing can stop me now!" practically still ringing in my ears, I suited up the next morning and made my way to swim practice. But over the ensuing weeks, I found myself struggling to keep up with the older kids. The final straw was when a girl I really admired for her swimming prowess looked right at me as I hauled my scrawny eight-year-old body out of the pool and said, "You're slow."

I never did swim team again after that summer. And I tell you this childhood tale not to tell you that the girl who told me I was slow ended up robbing a convenience store later in life. Although what a great ending that would be to this story. I share it because this is one of the most on-brand stories I can share about my childhood—and it makes me realize there were patterns that were formed in me from my youngest days, such as:

- *Delusions of grandeur.* Yes. Why else would I have thought of myself as the Dorothy Hamill of swimming except without ice skates?
- *Self-doubt when I wasn't automatically the best.* Yes. Am I Tina Fey? Then why am I even writing a book?
- *Quoting something from a line I heard on a TV show because I thought it sounded dramatic and cool.* Of course. I still do this. Perry and I are watching *Narcos* right now, and I recited the breakfast menu at our favorite Mexican food breakfast place the other morning like I was Pablo Escobar ordering chilaquiles with flour tortillas on the side.
- *Allowing someone else to make me feel like I wasn't good enough, which only confirmed my suspicions that I wasn't good enough.* Check and check.
- *Quitting without ever really seeing what I could do, because it's better to quit than to work hard and maybe fail.* Yes. If at first you don't succeed, it's probably better to just quit. Just like you see on all those motivational posters in business offices.

In my teenage years, I did this exact same quit thing with the high school dance team. I'd tried out for cheerleader at the beginning of my freshman year and didn't make it. I had been a cheerleader in eighth grade, so I was devastated as only a girl who'd once known the glory of doing a herkie jump in front of the whole junior high can be. At the end of freshman year, they were holding tryouts for the dance team, and I had planned to try out. But in the end, I faked a knee injury because I was too afraid I wouldn't make it, and it seemed like the easiest way out. This feels like a good time to apologize to my parents for the money they spent on a pointless MRI to diagnose a non-existent knee condition.

It's a pattern I have fought my whole life. You know how people say, "When the going gets tough, the tough get going"? I have often fallen in the category of, "When the going gets tough, maybe I'll just lie down and take a nap."

But here's the kicker. As much as my tendency has been to let myself quit or give up or walk away, there is also something in me as I've grown older that makes me want to fight that impulse. I don't want to give in to what others think of me or even to what *I* think of me because that's the one that can be the most damning of all.

A while back, Caroline started asking me questions about her nose. Did I notice that her nose was big? Did I see that it wasn't a button nose or even a ski slope nose? Why didn't she have a dainty, petite nose? I finally asked, "Who told you that you had a big nose?" She looked at me for a few seconds before naming a girl in her history class who'd told her exactly that. I pulled her close and had her look me in the eyes as I said, "You are beautiful. You are fearfully and wonderfully made, and your nose isn't a ski slope or button nose, but it fits your face and makes you exactly who you were created to be."

And you know what it made me think about? How the serpent tricks Eve, and then Adam, into eating the fruit from the tree of life. Their eyes are immediately opened to things they didn't know before, and so when God calls for them, Adam replies, "I heard you in the garden, and I was afraid because I was naked; so I hid." To which God responds, "Who told you that you were naked?" (Genesis 3:10–11). God hadn't created them with that insecurity. He knew they'd been told something that shifted what they knew and believed about themselves.

No matter how confident we are, I believe that deep down, we all have a voice that wants to whisper to us that we're a fraud or we'd be better if we were like this person or that person. Our voice is too loud, our laugh is too shrill, we are slow when we swim the fifty-meter butterfly. We'll never be a good writer or a good wife or a good mom. We don't know how to be a good friend or how to make a difference in our world. We are selfish, we are small, we are insignificant. That's what the voice says. For some of us, that voice is a real person in our lives, and for others, it's just our internal fear and doubt. For most of us, it's usually a combination of both.

The bottom line is that we can start to believe we aren't good enough, even though we are exactly who God meant for us to be. If that voice can make us believe lies about ourselves, then we'll spend the rest of our days trying to be something we were never created to be and wonder why we never feel content or satisfied.

✴ ✴ ✴

I mentioned earlier that Perry and I have been watching the series *Narcos* on Netflix. It's all about the rise of the drug cartels in Colombia starting in the 1970s, and while I find it to be fascinating, I feel the need to warn you that shows about drug cartels are not a feel-good endeavor, nor are they appropriate viewing for anyone under the age of twenty-one. But here's what we've noticed. These men, like Pablo Escobar, start off with nothing. They are born into poverty yet go on to have wealth beyond their wildest dreams. Granted, it's from smuggling cocaine, but they are living a life they could have never imagined, complete with mansions and cars and every luxury. Yet all those things cease to be enough. They continue to want more and more until it ultimately ruins them. Not a single one of their stories has a redemptive ending.

I realize it may be a stretch to compare my life to the head of a Colombian cartel, except for how we both launder things. I launder our clothing and they launder billions of dollars. But I'm going to need you to bear with me while I make this point come full circle. Thank you in advance.

When my first book was published back in 2012 and then hit the *New York Times* bestseller list, that was more than I could have ever comprehended. Let's remember that I was the kid who quit a neighborhood swim team because she didn't feel good enough, so the fact that I managed to write a blog for six years, which led to finding a literary agent, which led to finding a publisher, which led to having a book on the bestseller list was a pretty phenomenal accomplishment. I'd finally found something, other than being a wife and mother, that made me want to work hard at whatever it took to succeed.

Once the book came out, I began to get invitations to speak at events, and I eagerly accepted all of them because that felt like an important component of being a speaker and an author. People talked to me about building my "brand" and expanding my "platform," so I did my part to do all of those things. But at the end of twelve months, I began to realize I was chasing after something that wasn't ever going to fill me up. I was tired of airports and lonely hotel rooms and eating Cheez-Its out of a vending machine at 10:00 p.m. when I finished a speaking event. It had all looked so glamorous and exciting on the outside, but it felt totally different once I was in it.

I began to realize that my heart felt most content inside the walls of my house and surrounded by the people I love the most in the world. I didn't care if a lot of people knew my name or read my books because what mattered most to me was being at Caroline's homeroom parties, watching her play soccer on the weekends, and eating dinner as a family. I very consciously and prayerfully made the decision to accept a limited number of speaking engagements and quit worrying about things like a platform or brand. I realized that, for me, success wasn't really getting my name on some list as much as it was focusing on what God was doing in my house and with my friends and in my neighborhood and community. Don't get me wrong; the other stuff felt good, and I will flat out use *"New York Times* bestselling author" in my bio from now until the end of time. It's just not the thing that fills me up and makes me whole. My wholeness comes from knowing Jesus and trusting that he will always have me exactly where he wants me to be, speaking into the lives he wants me to impact.

And while I have not once regretted my decision, especially as I'm staring right down the barrel of being an empty nester, there are still times when the insecurities and the questions rise up, and I have to fight like Shammah for who and what God created me to be. Have you heard of Shammah? I'm guessing probably not because he just barely gets a mention in the Bible.

In 2 Samuel 23, we read about the end of King David's life and then see a list of David's mighty warriors, the men who were his special forces and constantly defended and fought for Israel. Almost hidden in the middle of this list is a story about how the Philistines decided to attack the Israeli army in the middle of this field of lentils. The Israeli troops fled, but one man named Shammah chose to take a stand right there in that field and defend it, even though common sense says that a wide-open bean field probably isn't an optimal place to engage in a battle, especially when the odds are stacked against you. There is no hiding place, no shelter, no place to avoid the battle. Not to mention that it was literally only a hill of beans.

But Shammah didn't back down. I believe that's because he knew it was a battle worth fighting, and that any ground he gave up to the enemy, no matter how insignificant it seemed, was going to be ground he'd have to fight like hell to get back at some point, or accept that it was gone forever.

There comes a time in our lives when we have to stand up and fight instead of backing down. We have to fight to be true to ourselves in a world that wants to tell us we have to be something we're not. We have to fight for our families. We have to fight where God has called us to step in and make a difference. There is ground in our life that we have to choose to defend. At times, it may seem that the ground we are called to protect may not be that important, but that very ground is the ministry, the calling, the family, the path that God has given us, and he has a plan and purpose for all of it. One of the greatest tricks the enemy can play on us is to convince us nothing is worth the fight. We have to hold our ground and remember that anything worth having is going to require taking a stand and not backing down.

And here's the best part. Shammah took his stand in that field of lentils, but it was God who gave him victory. Shammah's faith was never in his own ability to fight the battle or to accomplish great things; his faith was in the fact that God was with him.

The key to fighting for who and what you were created to be is remembering that the outcome isn't ultimately up to you. Believing that everything you are or are meant to accomplish is totally in your hands is exhausting because, frankly, we aren't that great. Maybe that's what I should have titled this book: *Girl, You Ain't That Great.*

We get tired, frustrated, short-sighted, and selfish. We will want to quit the swim team when it gets hard, because life takes more gumption than we are often able to muster on our own, especially when it's time to pull on our big girl pants and face it. Feeling like it's all up to us to create this thing or build that dream or achieve this goal is only allowing ourselves to be less than we were meant to be, and that's not freedom.

You were made for more. You are deeply loved and thought-fully created. I once read an interpretation of the phrase "fearfully and wonderfully made" from Psalm 139 that said your creation moved God to his deepest emotion. That's how much your exist-ence was thought out, that's how intricately you were made, and it makes sense that it's only as you go where he leads you that you experience real contentment and real joy.

A few weeks ago, it was an ordinary Saturday night at my house while a big women's Christian conference was going on elsewhere. I'd seen the posts about it on social media, and sometimes that stuff triggers my feelings of not being good enough and feeling left out. I sat in my kitchen, wearing the pajamas I'd been in since 4:00 p.m., and watched through the windows as Perry grilled burgers in the backyard. I poured myself a glass of wine, turned on my Spotify mix of acoustic cover songs, which I knew he and Caroline would make fun of later, and put on my new reading glasses that make me look like Harry Caray. And I realized there was nowhere else in the world I'd rather be in that moment. For a girl who grew up dreaming of family and stability, this is the good stuff. This is my dream come true, and God knew that about me. He showed me what was worth the fight.

The bright side is, he loves us enough to lead us to exactly who he made us to be, and to give us victory when we stand our ground and fight to stay true to ourselves in a world that will tell us all the ways we need to change.

CHAPTER 16

THINGS THAT HELP US

SEE THE
BRIGHT SIDE

So now that you're at the end of this book, you might find yourself wondering how you find the bright side. Here's a list of things that are my bright side, although I'm sure there are many others I'm forgetting. As I told the guy at Discount Tire the other day when he asked if my car had self-locking lug nuts, "You'd be shocked at all the things I don't know."

1. Putting myself in a time-out. Seriously. Sometimes when I am spiraling, I just need a few minutes to myself to be quiet, pray, or just hear myself think.

2. Having dinner planned and the necessary groceries bought more than thirty minutes before it's time to actually eat dinner.

3. Remembering to buy everything on my list at the grocery store. Or, better yet, grocery delivery.

4. The first day of fall, when the air is finally cool after a long, hot summer.

5. Seeing an Amazon Prime package on my front doorstep when I get home.

6. Organizing my closet and throwing out things I don't wear anymore.

7. Doing laundry in a timely and efficient manner and actually putting it away. Or, better yet, getting Caroline to put it away.

8. Listening to my friends tell stories about what's going on in their lives, because I have funny friends.
9. Reading glasses. I am forty-eight. This is my reality. They help me see everything better.
10. How excited Piper and Mabel are to see me every time I come home.
11. Dodging a stomach virus after everyone else in the family has had it.
12. Mexican food and a margarita on Friday nights.
13. Not having to make small talk.
14. Eating healthy and exercising on a regular basis. I will work out one time, eat a salad, and decide I look and feel better.
15. When I'm able to resist buying things online, especially when they look so great on my favorite fashion bloggers.
16. Buying things online that turn out to be better and cuter than I thought. I am not a superhero, just a woman who sometimes has no willpower.
17. When I quit worrying about things I can't control.
18. The nights I go right to sleep and sleep through the night. Thanks for that, melatonin.
19. The first cup of coffee in the morning.
20. Seeing Caroline do the right thing when she doesn't know I'm paying attention. It's those moments when you think maybe they're listening after all.

It's All About the Small Things

Why the Ordinary Moments Matter

Melanie Shankle

In *It's All About the Small Things*—formerly titled *Church of the Small Things*—Melanie Shankle helps you embrace what it means to live a simple, yet incredibly meaningful life and how to find all the beauty and laughter that lies right beneath the surface of every ordinary, incredible day.

Is my ordinary, everyday life actually significant? Is it okay to be fulfilled by the simple acts of raising kids, working in an office, and cooking chicken for dinner?

It's been said, "Life is not measured by the number of breaths we take, but by the number of moments that take our breath away." The pressure of that can be staggering as we spend our days looking for that big thing that promises to take our breath away. Meanwhile, we lose sight of the small significance of fully living with every breath we take.

Melanie Shankle, *New York Times* bestselling author and writer at *The Big Mama Blog*, tackles these questions head on. Easygoing and relatable, she speaks directly to the heart of women of all ages who are longing to find significance and meaning in the normal, sometimes mundane world of driving carpool to soccer practice, attending class on their college campus, cooking meals for their family, or taking care of a sick loved one.

The million little pieces that make a life aren't necessarily glamorous or far-reaching. But God uses some of the smallest, most ordinary acts of faithfulness—and sometimes they look a whole lot like packing lunch.

Available in stores and online!